The Führer, the Ariosophs, and the Third Global Catastrophe

Johannes H. von Hohenstätten

www.hermeticleague.com
hermeticleague@gmail.com

Creation of the cover, layout and additional material
by Peter Windsheimer
Original German title *Die Wahrheit **über** den Führer, die Ariosophen
und die dritte Weltkatastrophe*

Disclaimer

Content

Introduction by Peter Windsheimer

Resulting from the event of this new pandemic, the spread of a SARS-CoV-2 (Novel Coronavirus) that traveled across the globe at high speed, I have decided to translate this work, which was initially published in 2016 and revised in 2017.

Up to now, we have taken many things within our societies for granted and enjoyed constant economic growth and developed an ever-increasing taste for consumer goods. We have been spoiled with the newest gadgets available on a market that conjectures that the sky is the limit. In the times that I grew up, people held on to things much longer. If the TV or your radio had broken, you brought it to a repair shop. Albeit life had been "simpler," consumerism began to spread rapidly after World War II.

After the last World War, and all the carnage and suffering left an impression on the generation of my parents. Understandably, people wanted to enjoy life again, be happy, and find a meaning to live again.

However, both World Wars had set causes in motion that show their effects in this new millennium. Instead of frugally enjoying the fruits of our labor more modestly, our society went overboard acquiring more that we need or can enjoy without forgetting our purpose of developing as spiritual beings. Even religions have become materialistic havens for elitism and exclusion. Religious fundamentalism has distorted the original messages of the various founders of religions. Especially in the West, Christianity is being used to justify materialism, nationalism, and supremacy.

Most religions have become ghostly shadows of their original intentions and become decomposing carcasses given the illusion by embalming them through pride in national accomplishments and a false sense that a God favors one nation over another. Many eastern religions travel the same dark roads that Christianity travels as a whole. A false belief in a Creator God who would favor an individual based on faith alone, has developed a dangerously false sense of security. The followers of such faiths are desensitized to wholesome destruction of our environment and waste of natural resources, believing that they will be forgiven by a supreme being, neglecting to reflect on the laws of cause and effect. These laws reign in our physical world and the spiritual realm as well.

The beginning of the year 2020 has given us an excellent opportunity to slow down our fast-paced way of life and divert from economic greed, laissez-faire capitalism, and complacency, be become humble and lead more frugal lives away from excessive consumerism. If we do not begin to reflect on our way of life and begin to change from within, karma will show us the way in a very unpleasant way.

Peter Windsheimer

Boca Raton, FL; April 2020

Prologue

One may question the need for another book about Hitler, occultism, and the Third Reich by this little-known author? That is a justified question. However, most literature on this subject has been written partly by authors who misinterpreted the material out of ignorance. So much material was copied, and over time, this information became distorted or deliberately falsified to further confuse the readers. Furthermore, one must consider the fact that Adolf Hitler was one of the greatest liars and deceivers in history. Everything around him was smoke and mirrors, glitter, and pretenses.

This book attempts to shed some light on the inner workings of Hitler and his surroundings and will reveal the truth about his so-called occult dabbling. Once put into perspective, the events behind the scene played out quite differently. Official accounts of Hitler's occult life were all observed from a different angle, and occult research did not get far. The reader may be familiar with the books by Miguel Serrano and other writers of Hitler and the occult. Serrano revered Hitler as a godlike individual who had the mission to reshape the world. Albeit, Hitler would never have been able to achieve such a position. This author is completely addicted to the myth of this "Aryan" world leader.

I sought advice from my friend and mentor, Anion (Seila Orienta), in reference to the complex mechanisms of politics and lodges that ultimately had inspired me to write this book! Anion's wife Ariane confirmed these statements more than once, and she supplied me with further information which I implemented in writing. I am not concentrating on politics, but rather reflect on the working lodges and orders behind the scenes of the Third Reich. Of the many secret orders that existed at the time of

Hitler's rise to power, very few exerted any real influence on the political decisions in Germany and other countries in the past and present. All this I will openly present in this small book.

I will more closely examine the true relationship between Franz Bardon and Adolf Hitler. As stated in Frabato, Hitler had Bardon imprisoned in a concentration camp for non-compliance. Furthermore, I will also touch upon the life of Adolf Hitler, who, contrary to popular belief, was not well trained in the occult arts. Hitler's occult expertise was distorted and exaggerated, either deliberately or unconsciously, to further obscure his persona. Franz Bardon's student, Otti Votavova, who absolved the training of the 1st Tarot Card and began practicing evocations, had ultimately faltered in her training due to some hidden destructive personality traits. During numerous meetings, Otti Votavova told Dieter Rüggeberg that Hitler had been a member of the FOGC. This is a fundamental misstatement caused, among other things, controlling schemes (elementals) to plagued Otti Votavova in later years. Her statements and other speculations on Hitler's occult abilities created a myth of an invincible leader, hero, and almost a god-like persona who reigned over the masses.

Rather than fueling a Führer myth and this work points out Hitler's real weaknesses as a person, his tendency to sadism, and his sheer boundless narcissism and sociopathy. All of Hitler's characteristics can be summed up into one cause: the sex drive. It may interest students of the hermetics to see how such a monstrous persona proceeded to power, and how such a fragile character managed to be cheered and elevated to become an absolute ruler of one of the most powerful and technologically advanced nations at the time. Hitler only managed to reach his goals and carry out his mission with the aid of a high ranking and mighty demonic entity. Initially, this book bore the title *Adolf Hitler, the Ariosophs, and the Third World War from a Hermetic Perspective.* Owed to newly ascertained facts, Adolf Hitler had never been an expert of the occult and therefore could not have been the only authority without tireless assistance by diabolic entities.

There will not be such a Third World War that so many „prophets" and „psychics anticipated, in which a mighty Hitler had some involvement through cause and effect.

After writing and publishing the original manuscript, I had an intense conversation with my friend and advisor, Ariane, who conveyed this new information, which I included in this new edition. Initially, I also fell for old myths of a healthy, disciplined, influential leader. First, Hitler's speeches, his behavior, gestures, and appearance fascinated me and captivated me. I must openly admit that. Secondly, I subscribed to the myth that Hitler was well versed in the occult practices, a genuine master of the left path, and a high-ranking member in dark, secret societies.

Additionally, I had gathered so much published non-occult statements about the causes of an imminent global war called the Third World War. However, there will be a global catastrophe that should be titled "New Age" since this forthcoming series of events will awaken many individuals that Socrates titled „sleepwalkers." The signs point to the events that are favorable for such a catastrophe.

There is also a great misconception that occult order and secret societies comprise of capable magicians and quabbalists [sic] who wield supernatural powers. These orders accord the impression that all members are magically gifted. This conception has been deliberately publicized to fabricate a false impression of authority. Sometimes, the biggest lies appear to be truths when repeated incessantly. There are only very few orders that have some high-ranking members that are magically well-trained individuals whose numbers are minute. These extremely exceptional members are publicly unknown and always operate incognito. Orders that have such influential members are categorically closed societies, whereto very few exceptionally talented individuals have access to receive excellent training. Ariane accurately stated that loge members who boast their abilities are truly inept.

Johannes J. von Hohenstätten

Introduction

There is a common consensus among many people who study the occult that formidable black-magic lodges and orders determine, stage, and trigger wars. However, there is only one brotherhood that may authorize set the causes for such events, namely „The Brotherhood of Light." Bardon adverts to this brotherhood in his novel Frabato, and so does the theosophist Annie Besant.

The Blue Monks – as the members are often referred to – set the causes, and dispense their orders to the appropriate negative beings from all spheres. Then these beings bestow their orders upon individual adept members of lodges – such as Gregor A. Gregorius or Grandmaster Giovanni – who carry out these orders in the material world. The Blue Monks sometimes set causes that were not intended by Divine Providence and universal laws. Since the brethren are god-like beings, they may create causes outside the evolutionary scope. One must note that all this is accomplished in the spirit of harmonious development, and the brethren will naturally compensate to prevent chaos.

However, as seen from the perspective of the dark orders, the members are the chosen ones. They prepare conflicts and wars in a way that these members benefit from those actions. Today's political situation of the EU directly reflects the conditions created by Hitler's regime. The expansion of the European Union's economic domination that first has overtaken Europe naturally strives to expand beyond its boundaries. This development will not bode well. The USA follows a similar path as it desires world domination economically and by force while securing bases all over the world. Politicians all over the world are obsessed with power that will be the dynamic cause for a global collapse.

The reunification of East and West Germany in 1990 had caused protests from all over the world. The citizens of many nations feared that Germany would attempt to regain its formal prowess. Germany has become the most dominating economic force within the E. U. and applies its economic will within the European economic sphere of influence. Ultimately, only the upper echelon of society benefits financially (in the USA, they are known as the upper 0.1%), although most of those are unaware of the underlying causes. Ultimately, this avarice and greed will lead to the demise of society, from the ruling class down to the working poor.

1.
History

Both previous world wars were arranged and staged by great lodges and orders such as the FOGC and the Nordic Thule Order and others. US America and Soviet Russia – capitalism and communism – were mere lodge experiments that originated in Germany.

These were necessary steps to advance to a „Novo Ordo Seculorum," a new world order that is based on harmony and equality. Since everything must be destroyed sooner or later, wars, social upheaval, and economic collapses are the inevitable steps to an efficient world order. Thus Shiva destroys matter, so that we who are blinded by consumerism and social strive, recognize Maya, the great deception.

At the beginning of the 20th century, innumerable occult lodges and associations emerged in the German-speaking countries. These groups flooded the entire occult scene and conveyed their ideas, views, and philosophies to the public through countless occult magazines. Over forty magazines were covering all occult themes that exist and have existed.

Thule Society

Many of the orders were of Nordic origin. The *Thule Gesellschaft* (Thule Society) and the *Fraternitas Saturni* based their teachings on an "Aryan" philosophy. It was the first and last time that black magical orders stood in the public eye to lure most capable of them, the most trained could be sorted out to find their way into the magical-

The "Aryan" type

ly working lodges. Hitler and his henchmen used the same tactics of these Masonic lodges for their purposes of directing the masses. The race ideology of race, blood, soil, space, and will was only the entrance gates, the first stages for the masses according to the principle of Julius Caesar's "Bread and games for the simple people."

Why did Germany become the ultimate victim in this world order? All the atrocities in the Middle Ages, the wicked burning of witches, which were mostly carried out in Germany, the first translation of the Bible from Latin, the printing technology, the philosophy, the land of poets and thinkers answer that question. Bardon sums this state by saying to his pupil Milan Kumar "Divine Providence has forsaken us. Lately, we live very comfortably."

2.
Enter the Pathological Führer
The Trickster

A historical examination of the great leader" Adolf Hitler's mental and physical health is not novel in itself, although some of the records that were kept by German psychiatrists have mysteriously disappeared. Hitler had become successful by naturally attracting a particular type of people. Some gullible individuals believed everything without scrutiny. Hitler captivated ignorant and uneducated individuals, as well as the less intelligent, the naïve, and impressionable youths and children through his personality and false charisma. Other groups included despots, thugs, sociopaths, brutal individuals, racists, bigots, and the asocial found a sympathetic leader in Hitler. Opportunists, psychopaths, and narcissists who recognized an opportunity to enrich themselves or move up in ranks and be admired by the masses for their feigned charisma, competence, and leadership, becoming a role model the typical German admired for his service of helping to build a great nation. The disadvantaged realized an opportunity to rise in ranks beyond their competence, and the capitalist upper echelon of society recognized prospects of significant financial gains, while militarists foresaw an expansion of their sphere of influence. Hitler had a natural aptitude for delivering visions that people want to hear, flattering the masses of Germany, painting pipe dreams, Illusions, and pretense. The masses were desperate for a new Germany, and Hitler banked on this desperation and fueled the fire of new hope in the hearts of people.

A successful dictator needs scapegoat, groups of people he will blame for all problems tnd deficiencies and incompetence a dictator might face. The Jews and communists presented an ideal group that Hitler used for his purposes. Eventually, the Nazis added other groups to serve the regime's purpose. The Jews and communists were blamed for the shameful defeat of Germany in the First World War. The industrial elite of Jews, the Jewish bankers purportedly played into the hands of an international enemy. At the same time, the growing regime condemned Communists for backstabbing society, attempting to create a state of anarchy and boycotting the military might of the prewar military machinery.

The war is his fault.
(Nazi caricature)

Hitler skillfully appealed to the purity of race, the superiority of the average German over the intellectual, and perceived racial impurity of Jewry. The true German worker and farmer had become the hero of making Germany great again. The proletariat enjoyed recognition by a – what they perceived – a great man and leader who understood their needs. The Führer emphasized and conserved time-honored traditions and ways of life of simpler times. By stressing a pure German spirit, purity in character and blood, the strong, invincible, the warrior man and the woman, the keeper of the home, hearth, and family appealed to many. On the other hand, he captivated to less ethical individuals by reciprocating their vises, and personality traits, and desensitizing broad masses to an eventual public display of injustice and violence against the "undesirables." Others who openly opposed the National Socialist cause were intimidated, incarcerated, or executed.

Hitler's adherents found an advocate who catered to people's emotions and convictions. A successful dictator strategically places himself at the head of the masses and poses as a capable genius, a moral compass, a benevolent and likable leader, a savior, and a God-like individual, chosen by Divine Providence, Hitler presented the shining light during dark times. Joseph Goebbels, Hitler's charismatic Minister of Propaganda, rightly stated that a "lie told repeatedly becomes the truth."

1. *Dolchstoßlegende (backstabbing).*
"German, do not forget"

2. *Death to Marxism march by the*
Nazis

Adolf Hitler, the former drifter, the sociopath, and criminal, has found a permanent place in history, and by the law of perseverance, his name will life on for generations and even today, new post World War II generations around the world admire Hitler's cause and his message. It is quite disturbing to see how this Nazi cult persevered and will continue to thrive for some time. All the atrocities that the otherwise harmless average German committed bases on the principle of cause and effect. Encourage an ordinary person time and again to commit acts of cruelty and give proper justification for immoral acts, and individuals will lose their natural conscience.[1] On a more transcendental level, the concepts, ideas, and thoughts that were placed by negative beings streamed from chosen "leader" who knew how to manipulate and influence the masses with a rare mastery of charisma corrupted the broad masses with ease. That pathetic being, Adolf Hitler, has placed himself at the top of a mighty nation.

Simultaneously, Hitler seemingly displayed indispensable abnormality, and even severe, pathological traits. His burning characteristics, which he validated during his speeches, but also the almost epileptoid sweeping gestures, catches the eye. Hitler and his most fervent followers saw in him an emissary of God, a chosen one who had is adversaries ruthlessly put to death. He reveled in the spectacle trials lead by judge Roland Freisler at the trials of the defendant accused of involvement in the assassination attempt of July 20, 1944. Most were hanged, a humiliating dishonorable way of execution for soldiers, and, according to the eyewitness reports, the victims' trousers were pulled down while dying on makeshift gallows and piano wires. Some were slowly released to prolong the agony. The spectacle was filmed for Hitler's enjoyment.

Dr. Georg Lomer, M.D. stated that during Hitler's reign, most Germans sooner or later recognized the inherent evil and demonic traits emanating from their glorious leader who claimed that Divine Providence had sent him to make Germany shine. Hitler was never a robust and healthy individual in the body and mind. His real power lies in the secret of the root chakra and its utilization in the practice of sexual magic. The arousal of the Mulad-

---

[1] *See the „Stanford-Prison-Experiment" conducted by behavioral psychologists in 1971.*

hara center can be achieved through diverse methods, either through sexual stimulation or violence. Therein lies the cause for the indescribable human sacrifices, where millions of human beings are violently slaughtered or worked to death at concentration camps. Millions more fell victim to warfare. Brutal warfare in Russia and the nihilation of whole armies caused intense arousal of Hitler's root chakra, and the forces that he harvested were, among other things, the reason for his stranglehold over the German people and other nations by submission.

However, this psychopath, and servant to demonic forces seemed irredeemably unsatisfied. Hitler was consumed by an unbearable inner tensions, whose hoarse bellowing resembled the roar of wild animals or cave dwellers. This inner tension finds its cause in sexual pathology, the ancient breeding ground of humankind's most primitive, and vicious instincts. Bardon states in his second work in the chapter that outlines the Mars sphere *"The expert in astrology will know that the Mars sphere, in its effectiveness, prevailingly adheres to the Mars principle, for passionate love, eroticism, supernatural power of man, wars, etc., are owed to the influence of the Mars sphere. For the reader's information it is pointed out in this connection that the negative intelligences living in the Sun and the Mars sphere are the most dangerous ones of our whole cosmic hierarchy. Under their range of effectiveness come: murder, rape, sexual deviation, robbery; arson, destruction of property, war, opression."*

Dr. Martha Vaerting, an early 20th century German sociologist, educator, and pioneer in gender study, drew attention to the fact that *"sickliness in men and women increases the belligerence."* She further states that *„The fiercest belligerents were mostly weak or deformed men. Homer Lea who suffered from a deformity of his spine clearly serves as an example. He foresaw the conflict be-*

tween the USA and Japan in his writings and glorified warfare and military doctrines and sought to fulfill his martial desires. Clearly, this sort of physical frailty has a provocative and, in a certain sense, degenerative effect on the sexuality of those affected. There is a considerable range of potentials, from simple mania to a predatory type of perversion. A mass murderer like Fritz Haarmann[2] who, after sex and subsequent murder would dissect his victims and sell their meat as veal. Such an individual can hardly be considered to be sexually normal. Compare these acts committed by Haarmann to warfare were young men are slaughtered in bloody frenzies. The parallels between abnormal sexuality and violence, are obvious."

All the above statements were corroborated by my friend and adept Ariane; otherwise I would never mention in this book.

Adolf Hitler's birthplace, Braunau, was astrologically speaking a center for mediums, pathological characters, and psychopaths. Alois Hitler regularly beat his son, Adolf, after arriving home drunk. This trauma positively triggered some of Hitler's latent psychopathic traits later in life.

The seemingly asexual Hitler had a pathological sex drive and was obsessed with power and authority. Sex, dominion, and violence often complement each other as it was the case with Hitler. Practicing sexual magic rituals augmented his grip over others since a sexual act, when harnessed expertly, releases vast amounts of energy that the magician can impregnate with any wishes. When

---

[2] *Fritz Haarmann (1879-1925), called the „Werewolf of Hannover," was convicted and sentenced to death for the murder of 27 boys and young men. He used to pick up his victims and had sex with them. During the sexual act, he developed an uncontrollable urge to bite the throat of his subjects.*

young Hitler had come to Vienna in 1907, he found one of the great cultural centers of Europe before the First World War. Aside from art, music, science, and literature, Vienna had also become a center of mysticism and secret societies. Psychology and parapsychology had their birthplace in Vienna. The Viennese physician, Sigmund Freud, created new theories in his sexual psychology, although many have been debunked by modern psychology. However, the sex drive remains the primal power of humankind, which Hitler should have studied more closely.

At Hitler's arrival in Vienna, there was a strong aura that emanated occultism and spread its influence through Europe. The runologist Lanz von Liebenfels who hoisted a swastika flag on the *Werfenstein Castle*, the headquarters of his order *Ordo Novi Templi*. The *Theosophical Society* had a significant presence in Austria's capital. One notable member was Rudolf Steiner, who later founded the *Anthroposophical Society*. Furthermore, the Austrian politician, writer, and occultist, Lazar von Hellenbach and the German Karl du Prel held seances in Vienna. The Austrian occultist Karl Brandler-Pracht founded an astrological society in Vienna. Guido von List and Lanz von Liebenfels also spread the concept of an "Aryan" occult system that found in a culturally diverse Vienna, appealed to many anti-semitic Austrians.

Ordo Novi Templi

While living in Vienna, Hitler read everything he could obtain on about the occult, even though, according to his statement in his autobiography, *Mein Kampf*, he was penurious, starving, and could not afford much, despite receiving two pensions. Hitler's statement of his condition was just one of the countless lies that served him well during his rise to power. According to Lanz von Liebenfels, Hitler had contact with the *Ordo*

Novi Templi. The Viennese psychologist and author, Wilfried Daim, claimed that Liebenfels inspired Hitler and transposed his philosophies on Hitler. Daim's claim is correct since Hitler was not able to think innovatively or creatively on his own. One example of his lack of creativity is the expansion of the Autobahn in North Rhine-Westphalia, for which he took credit. However, the plans for expansions existed before Hitler presumably drafted his "own" plans. Another example is the "Hitler Salute" or "Sieg-Heil Salute." Hitler had borrowed the salute of raising one's right arm to neck height and straightened arm from Italy's fascist leader Benito Mussolini who, in turn, borrowed the salute from the Romans (Saluto Romano).

Hitler lived a block away from the headquarter of the *List Society* and was allegedly a member of it. This society propagated a nationalistic philosophy that was influenced by List's books on runes, ancient Teutonic culture, and purity of race. His membership of the *List Society* allowed Hitler to make further contacts with other lodges, he wanted and had to, because he was looking for power he never had himself. The Germanic League *Walhalla* also tried to coerce Hitler to join. During his time in Vienna, Hitler had close ties to various orders that had many German members. Contacts to Germans opened new possibilities and opportunities for Hitler. Through his contacts with various orders, Hitler gathered some, if only sparse information about the infamous *FOGC* (Freemason Order of the Golden Century [Century = Number 100]).

By 1917, Germanic occult orders were founded everywhere. All of them possessed evocative old Germanic names, but all these orders became merely receptive orders for a dominant Nordic order. This order pursued other goals than merely political ones. Some members of this high order had missions to transform political arenas. The *Thule Society* was only a more publicly open occult society. Whereas, the actual *Thule Order* (note the difference between "Society" and "Order"), the unknown secret order only accepted real occult experts who conducted evocations of negative genii. Naturally, Hitler, who was not an authentic expert in occult matters, became only a member of the *Thule Society* and not the *Thule Order.*

Hitler also read the complex and somewhat perplexing and eccentric works of Aleister Crowley. Although Crowley undoubtedly had magical powers, however, his appetite for drugs wreaked havoc on his matrices and caused a steady degradation of his character, intellect, and morality.

For a time, Hitler lived in a boardinghouse for men where, as some biographers suspect, he used the opportunity to practice public speaking in front of many involuntary listeners. August Kubizek, a close friend of Hitler, allegedly had to listen to his rants and monologues as they often shared a room. Hence, Hitler never retired before three or four o'clock in the morning. These circuitous rants that revolved around the same topics must have driven Kubizek almost insane. Hitler had no original ideas or concepts to offer. His lackluster paintings are an excellent example of his character, as they were devoid of any personal style.

In 1913, Hitler fled the Hapsburg empire to Germany to avoid the draft. Tedious military drills and serving in an army that harbored soldiers from diverse ethnicities. Arrested in Munich and sent back to Austria, Hitler was also considered to be unfit at the physical examination, resulting from his poor general condition. While in Germany, he lived in squalid conditions owed to a lack of financial means in Germany. Hitler later served in the

German army, where he passed his physical exam, probably since he had recovered from his poor general condition. However, Hitler's family doctor certified that his health had never been seriously in disorder. One can see that much of his biography has been misinterpreted, partially because of speculation, and falsely imputed events.

In occult matters, Hitler desired to find his own path, but due to his lack of natural talent, he merely became an interpreter and medium for his demonic God. He dabbled in occult things, aided by the zeitgeist. For this reason, Hitler desired to get acquainted with various orders, appropriate their secrets and power, and utilize these for his purposes.

3.
Hitler's "Occult Acquaintances

Hitler's acquaintance, The German professor, general and politician, Karl Haushofer, was an expert on East Asia and traveled extensively to Tibet, India, and Japan. During his journeys, he familiarized himself with many secret societies, among others, Lama Trebisch-Lincoln's[3] *Society of the Green.* In order to be accepted into the order of the Green Dragon Society[4] (GDS) in Japan, he had to undergo severe trials. Haushofer found racial relations between Tibet and the Teutons. Haushofer founded an order that bore Tibetan characteristics. The Gelugpa (Yellow Hat Sect), founded by the fifth Dalai Lama, has a secret secondary branch that schooled black magic students of the FOGC (also called the Ninety-Nines). The Yellow Hat Sect, or namely, its secret branch was involved unseen in the machinations of World War II, like the Pentagram Order – Pentagon – which was infiltrated by members of the FOGC. Even in the Vatican entertained associations to this order.

Haushofer, who allegedly had demonstrable occult abilities, was a member of the earthly order of the „Brothers of Light,"[5] and magicians from all over the world belonged to this order, such as Buddhist, Shinto, Sufi, Rosicrucian, and shaman magicians. Additionally, during the National Socialist dictatorship, there existed a Tibetan colony in Berlin that maintained contact with a Tibetan

---

[3] *Ignatius* Timothy Trebisch-Lincoln *was Abbot Chao Kung*

[4] *Also known as „The Greens" or „The 72 Unknown Superiors."*

[5] *The term „earthly light" is soften associated with the negative Godhead Lucifer, the Bringer of Light.*

monastic order. This shows that occult lodges and orders are interconected globally.

An SS expedition to Tibet in 1938-39, built a radio station in the Tibetan capital of Lhasa to establish a radio connection between Lhasa and Berlin. If Hitler had been adept in occult matters, he would not have needed to communicate via radio. Rudolf Heß,[6] Hitler's Deputy Führer and a confidant of Hitler, was nicknamed the Yogi from Egypt." He was a member of several orders and a high-grade freemason. Nevertheless, these ranks and grades were all empty designates, and Heß possessed no occult controls. Rudolf Heß planned his flight to Scotland on an astrologically highly favorable time to no avail. The elite combat echelon, the SS, indoctrinated its members into occult matters. One division was called the skull and crossbones division (SS-Totenkopf-Division), not only because they spread death and destruction, but because they had sacrifice up their self by becoming part and parcel of a larger unit, a mere cog in the mechanisms of the SS. The SS borrowed this concept from the Buddhist teaching that Atta (true self) transforms to seek non-self (absence of a separate self) to connect to the cosmos.

Deputy Führer
Rudolf Heß

Unfortunately, Hitler has twisted this concept to serve only him by building an antlike army where the individual becomes dispensable if needed and be replaced by a new unit.

Some sources state that Georges Gurdjieff, the well-known Russian occultist, had been a member of a powerful black-magic lodge. Anion (Seila Orienta)

---

[6] Heß was later sentenced to death in absentia by Hitler for his flight to Scotland in 1941; thus, committing treason.

mentioned that Gurdjieff had been merely a candidate for the *Thule Order*, thus, only a member of the *Thule Society*. All well-trained people know these magical orders. Gurdjieff supposedly has been engaged as an occult spy, like Aleister Crowley and Theodor Reuss, the former head of the *Ordo Templi Orientis*. Gregor A. Gregorius' occult novel *The Path to Dark Light* discusses the subject of occult espionage and its influence. However, the fact remains that even the most potent black magicians do not possess real powers, were it not for their allied demons. These Elohim of the negative spheres only give their protégés what Divine Providence commends. These negative Elohim would be dissolved should they disobey Divine Providence's strict directives.

According to a report in the German newspaper *Frankfurter Allgemeine,* Hitler's plane was found in the jungle of northern Argentina. Some of his confidants testified in various documentaries on television that before the Russian closed in on the capital, many planes had taken off for the West – South America. The ARD (German television network, Channel 1) foreign correspondent Karl Brugger states in his book *The Chronicle of Akakor* that Hitler's single-handed military decisions, his plans for world conquest, and the actions of secret commands in the most distant parts of the world, such as Argentina and Brazil, were inscrutable. No one knew for what purpose these commands were established. Eyewitnesses claim to have observed the arrival of German submarines off the coast of Rio de Janeiro and Argentina. A reporter of the Brazilian magazine *Realidade* even discovered a German colony in the Brazilian state of Mato Grosso that consisted exclusively of former SS members. Hitler possibly stayed there for some time. My great uncle, an Austrian SS officer, fled to Argentina and was sought by the Nazi hunter Simon Wiesenthal. The CIA secretly did not believe any statements that Hitler was deceased and issued a warrant that included a composite of his changed appearance. Several pictures were taken of Hitler, showing him once with a beard, another being bald. According to Franz Bardon, Hitler had his face surgically altered. A US American documentary showed that Hitler had spent the night in a specific hotel, and, accompanied by a woman, visited a local opera. Hitler expertly concealed himself. Secret passageways allowed him to enter other rooms to hold conferences with confidantes, without being seen in the open. Since he suffered from paranoia, bordering on insanity, Hitler took extra measures to hide. Ultimately, Hitler died in Argentina.

Herman Göring, Hitler's Reichsfeldmarschall (Imperial Field Marshal) and head of the Luftwaffe, purportedly mastered the four elements (see Franz Bardon), but owed to his morphine addiction, which he contracted in an Innsbruck hospital after Hitler's attempted coup d'état[7] through a bullet wound, he foolishly lost control of the elements. Göring's mother had contact with a Swedish esoteric secret society. Her example led to her son's interest in esotericism.

Wewelsburg and adjacent town

This edition of the book corrects what was written about Heinrich Himmler, Hitler's trusted head of the SS and

---

[7] *Beer Hall Putsch in November 1923.*

Black Sun Symbol. This symbolis golden colored when it is a positive sun symbol. The number 12 symbolizes evolution

executer of the *Final Solution* in his death camps. Himmler was a *Thule* master, a master of occult techniques. An antiquarian bookseller stated that Himmler had a private esoteric library in Hungary with thousands of books. Himmler even proclaimed that he remembered one of his previous incarnations, the East Francian king Heinrich I. (Henry the Fowler). He and his 12 vassals during rituals influenced individuals of power. Himmler also had the Wewelsburg Castle rebuilt according to his ideas. He had his cult room built with 12 stone seats, in the ceiling a swastika, and in the place above, there was a *Black Sun* laid in marble that comprised of twelve Sig-Runes (Sowelu). This castle became the seat of the *Thule Order.*

Black Sun (Schwarze Sonne) and crypt inside Wewelsburg Castle

Ahnenerbe logo. Written in pseud-runic letters: Deutsches Ahnenerbe.

(Credit: By Ahnenerbe.jpg: Co-flensderivative work: Malyszkz)

Hitler fancied to surround himself with like-minded people who wanted to exercise power, which is the real reason for the formation of the pseudo-scientific *Forschungsgemeinschaft Deutsches Ahnenerbe* (Research Association of German Ancestral Heritage), who searched the world for occult relics that were uniquely "Aryan" and pertaining to German heritage.

4.
Hitler's Obsession with Dominance

The ideology of the National Socialists dictated the establishment of a new form of religion and culture that suited the National Socialist spirit. This new culture and spiritualism should have replaced all previous religious systems. To this end, the state established a cult that ultimately undermined developed German culture to keep the masses away from influences outside the Nazi ideology. This way, Hitler and the upper echelon of Nazi greats profited from the complete assimilation of the nation's collective. Himmler founded the *Ahnenerbe* research department to pursue secret societies and their members who were suspected of being adepts in occult matters. This little-known and poorly studied special research department ordered the arrest of fortune-tellers, runologists, astrologers, occultists, healers, and magicians to elicit their techniques and assess their effectiveness. Himmler considered these supernatural abilities to be powerful weapons that may be utilized in consolidating the supremacy of the Third Reich.

Hitler believed that he could expand and consolidate his power for this power to succeed in conquest. The Franco-English writer and admirer of Hitler, Savitri Devi, states in her book *Hart wie Kruppstahl* (Sturdy as Krupp Steel) that Hitler acted in the primal sense; i.e., in full accordance with the eternal laws of rhythm and harmony, of being and non-being. So, all Masonic Lodges in Germany and German-occupied territories were closed, and their members arrested and sent to concentration camps for "re-education." Hitler attempted to conceal his insatiable lust for power and desire to be the supreme leader without equals. Therefore, he took the measure of eliminating anyone who would possibly cross his plane. He rightly believed that world history can be altered by a small elite; hence, he considered himself to be part of a small circle of initiates. Hitler's views were clearly expressed in the famous Nazi maxim: *Ein Volk, ein Reich, ein Führer* (one nation – people, one empire, one leader). As a megalomaniac, Hitler viewed himself to a supreme being a godlike man who dominated over all people, disregarding the fact that above hatred, revenge, avarice, greed, cruelty, and sociopathy. He was intoxication by the forces that acted from beyond in the darkest demonic spheres, something that he could conjure into the physical realm through his ability to act as a medium between that realm and the physical world. Owed to his blind desire for power and supremacy, Hitler completely disregarded the higher principles such as Christian love of one's neighbor, love for one's perceived enemies the other races of people. Forgiveness, a virtue that Christianity and other religions profess were replaced by revenge and violent restitution. A lack of intelligent, spiritual insight, and furthering divine attributes within the human race, lead to Hitler's ultimate downfall and the destruction of Germany. This was Hitler's mission to create a new and better Germany through death and destruction. He sacrificed the present for a nobler future.

The following Biblical statements clearly demonstrate a universal law that any being has to adhere to: „Be not deceived; God is not mocked: for whatsoever a man soweth, that shall he also reap.

For he that soweth to his flesh shall of the flesh reap corruption; but he that soweth to the Spirit shall of the Spirit reap life everlasting.

And let us not be weary in well doing: for in due season we shall reap, if we faint not."[8]

The Reichsführer SS, Heinrich Himmler, ordered the annihilation of Freemasonry while appropriating Freemasonry's valuable treasures. In all the occupied territories, the German *Sicherheitsdienst* (security service), intruded al meeting places of Freemasons, to uncover their archives and rituals. The SS Security Forces failed to retrieve much beneficial material because there is an entirely independent, and publicly unknown branch of institutional Freemasonry whose actions are shrouded in a veil of secrecy. Similarly, there is an inner circle of the *Golden Dawn*, designated as angle lodges. These members are the heirs to genuine hermetic initiation. A knowledge that the ancient masters handed down to the next generation of capable adepts. These authentic lodges carefully harbored their original rituals that are untraceable by the outsider.

One of many propaganda posters emphasizing the concept of a supreme leader

Albeit the upper Nazi echelon conjectured that they could assimilate the all of Europe into Nazi ideology and to help the Templars become a mighty financial power to dominate the world through the useless rituals appropriated from Freemasonry, they completely

---

[8] *Galatians 6:7-9*

ignored that fact that they did not possess the rituals that the secret branch of Freemasonry practiced. The *Ancestral Heritage Research Department* (Deutsches Ahnenerbe) was responsible for appropriating occult material everywhere to aid in the manipulation of the masses. Himmler was convinced that the manipulation of souls was not just the most effective means to win a war, but also the establishment of permanent authoritarian rule afterward. The end of the war in 1945 (May 8th; VE-Day), not all research has ended. A secret underground still directs its resources toward achieving dominion. The post-war reconstruction and prosperity rendered the average people ignorant and unwilling to think while pursuing simple pleasures without realizing that they are being manipulated by a secret class to aid in concocting sinister plans by these true leaders. The Roman rulers coined the motto "circem et panem," to keep the masses well-fed, entertained, ignorant, and mentally indolent.

Some members of the Heritage Department – Ahnenerbe – team who were assigned to practice weaponized occult powers, increasingly believed in Nordic traditions and Tibetan mysticism. The Heritage Department had even sent a special commando to Lhasa to investigate the secrets of the Tibetan mysticism and occult practices. The Third Reich spent massive amounts of money on revealing occult sciences while the USA spent its money on the construction of the first atomic bomb. The activities of The Heritage Department ranged from locating the origin of the "Aryan" race to extensive expeditions to the most remote parts of the world. Some actions of the German army might appear odd to the casual historian. For example: When the German *Wehrmacht* troops had to abandon Naples to the approaching Allied troops, Himmler ordered the gravestone of the last Hohenstaufen Kaiser, who was buried in Naples to be brought to Germany. Alternatively, when the Russians marched into Berlin, they found hundreds of nameless Tibetans and Indians who had fallen alongside German soldiers. However, according to the following report, The Heritage Department was sometimes successful in finding morsels of occult relics. The German esoteric magazine *Die andere Welt* (The Other World), published an interesting article, written by E. Maria Körner, (p.651-652), that deals with Hitler's obsession for occult relics.

The Secret of Hitler's Mandrake

By E. Maria Körner

„Hitler was by no means alone in believing in the effects of extrasensory influences among his prominent party comrades.

Apart from him, deputy Führer Rudolf Heß and the head of the SS and Gestapo, Heinrich Himmler, cohered to horoscopes, amulets, mascots, and talismans, as they were firmly convinced of the power of these forces.

Hitler was an avid reader of the works of the German novelist, Hanns Heinz Ewers. Above all, Ewers' book titled 'Mandrake' left a deep impression on Hitler. However, the mandrake legends, which first appeared in the Middle Ages, emphasize sexual magic.

By reading the books of romantic poet and novelist, E.T.A. Hoffmann, and the American writer of tales of mystery, horror and the macabre, Edgar Allen Poe, Hitler became familiar with occult phenomena during a stay in Berlin in 1926, where he also met the psychic Erik J. Hanussen. Hanussen was, above all, a master of magic, and influencing the masses. Like Franz Bardon, Hanussen performed countless magical events on stage. He also successfully taught Hitler the secrets of rhetoric and speech techniques. Much of Hanussen's work remains forever hidden in archives. The Ahnenerbe (Ancestral Heritage Department) took responsibility for this.

Hitler gradually gained confidence in his new teacher, who slowly but surely managed to influence the student politically to change his direction. This event did not escape the attention of the hidden Thule Order. Strangely, Hanussen stubbornly refused to calculate a horoscope for Hitler, despite repeated requests. It was only shortly before the end of 1932 that Hanussen complied with Hitler's request by sending Hitler an impregnated (hermetically charged) mandrake talisman, and a horoscope as a New Year's gift. The Führer had long wished for such a root of the man-shaped root of the mandragora plant, whereto the people attributed mysterious powers and healing effects. Hanussen had predicted Hitler's seizure of power (and the extreme consequences of the war) to the day, although no one would have thought it possible in the last days of December 1932. The horoscope stated, '... and then on the day before the end of the month, you are at your destination and turning point, namely on January 30, 1933.'

At the New Year's Eve celebrations at Obersalzberg (Hitler's retreat in the mountains near Berchtesgaden, Bavaria), the present party leaders were wrought by melancholy about the party's future. Only Hitler, trusting in Hanussen's prophecy, looked confidently into the future.

The mandrake was a stately forty-eight-centimeter (19 in.) root, while mandrake roots usually reach a length of ten cm (4 in.) tall, resembling a shriveled dwarf walking awkwardly with spread legs and outstretched arms. When Hitler had shown this strange figure to the later Reichsmarschall Göring, the latter directed the Führer's attention to the striking resemblance between this strange, shriveled shape of the root and the diminutive gaunt stat-

ure of the future Minister of Propaganda, Josef Goebbels. The latter was colloquially known as 'pint-size Teuton' (Schrumpfgermane) during the Third Reich.

Mephisto (Goebbels) considered this comparison a deadly insult. However, the actual reason reasons why Goebbels' intimate friend Count Wolf-Heinrich von Helldorff,[9] in his capacity as police chief, had the psychic Hanussen murdered by his men a few months later. Hanussen's body was found in a forest near Potsdam. Preliminary proceedings against an unknown perpetrator in connection with Hanussen's murder were discontinued soon afterwards. Under no circumstances was Hanussen removed on behalf of, or with the tacit acquiescence of Hitler, because the psychic's advice was far too valuable to him at that time.

Possession of the magic root gave the Führer at enough self-confidence and strength to make his decisions with somnambulistic certainty. What he did during the first seven years of his domination was crowned with success. Even the first two years of the war brought an unbroken chain of victories that nobody would have thought possible. Was the mysterious mandrake the pledge of this fairytale happiness?

Hitler kept the root in a locked and sealed box in his private safe. After that, suddenly, the tide turned, and the seven successful years passed.

On May 10th, 1941, Heß flew to England on a supposed peace mission with the United Kingdom.

This mission, by one of Hitler's closest companions, caused tremendous embarrassment for the Reich, especially since Operation Sea Lion, the planned invasion of the British isles, was imminent. Consequently, Hitler lost faith in the occult powers, prohibited all occult cir-

---

[9] *Helldorff was executed by the Nazis in 1944, following the assasination attempt on Hitler, due to his knowledge of the plan.*

cles and societies, and persecuted their members. Goebbels now took the opportunity to attempt to destroy Hitler's mandrake. Goebbels dispatched a high-ranking SS officer to Obersalzberg to destroy the box and mandrake on the spot.

Consequently, the officer did not obey his order and instead sent the mysterious object to a friend in Vienna, who was an avid collector of Hitler mementos and paintings.

On May 15th, 1941, the talisman was taken from Obersalzberg. On the same day, Hitler issued the directive to amass his troops on the eastern border and made the final preparations for his campaign against Russia, named Operation Barbarossa. This attack on Russia ended with the military collapse of German history and the fall of the Thousand-Year Reich.

When Hitler became aware of the disappearance of his talisman, Goebbels had to bear the brunt of one of Hitler's famous tantrums. The mandrake remained missing, for the Viennese collector had hidden it in a suitcase in the air-raid shelter of his house. Later this house was bombed out, and the cellar filled with rubble. After 1945, the suitcase was found amidst the rubble of the ruin. Miraculously, the mandrake had remained undamaged.

It was opened in the presence and under the control of a notary. The mandrake came out safely. A sealed silver capsule was enclosed in the neck of the root. It was opened, and two small parchment rolls fell out. Hanussen had written on them:

> *"... but woe begets when the covenant is broken,*
> *The evil word, once spoken.*
> *Then the spirit, of the titanic ward,*
> *Sinks to the Orcus into an abyss quite dark.*

All goes up in smoke and flames;
The cycle of twelve reaches for its claims.
The great spell as a binder,
Shall strike the owner and the finder,
And even once both shall find their demise,
The unscathed mandrake shall again arise.'

Fraud or falsification of the findings seems impossible. There is not the slightest doubt as to the authenticity of the mandrake and the associated prophecies of Hanussen. A protocol prepared by an attorney's (UK: barrister) affidavit is readily available."

5.
The Exploits of the Freemasonic Order of the Golden Century[10] (FOGC)

It should have been clear from the beginning that the FOGC would not allow its destruction by a member of its lodge. One word from the Grandmaster of the Lodge would have been enough to put a stop to Hitler. In this order, the powerful rites produce immediate effects. The Grandmaster of the Fraternitas Saturni, Gregor A. Gregorius – and some of the higher-ranked members – were all FOGC.

Gregorius confirms that there are magic lodges that work politically in the following excerpt from his unpublished novel *The Way into the Dark Light*:

Gregor A. Gregorius (Eugen Grosche), Grandmaster of the Fraternitas Saturni (Berlin)

„*The path led to occult circles and likely to secret circles that worked on influencing political events anonymously and unnoticed.*"

Furthermore, the use of sexual magic by certain secret circles – among others the Fraternitas Saturni – to influence political events. Through their rituals, they create causes that have the desired effects.

To emphasize the fact that sorcerers are expert liers, an article by Gregorius states

---

[10] *In this instance, „Century" connotes the number „One Hundred."*

that the FS distances itself from any political activities and party lines. Such a statement contradicts what he wrote in the above-cited novel: *"Our lodge does not engage in public politics and keep a neutral stance to political views. It is our idealistic goal that we distance ourselves as a lodge, from common political scuffles and political strife that predominates everyday life."*

Grandmaster Giovanni (Karl Wedler), one of Gregorius' acquaintance, worked at the public order office in Bochum (a city in North Rhine-Westphalia, Germany), met many influential people through his position, whom he inspected clairvoyantly and consequently influenced. After the publication of his novel *Auf Teufel komm raus* (Come Hell or High Water), he became the master of Bochum.

In the surrounding area of the St. Johannis hospital in Bochum, some mansions bear strange signs above their doors. One sign read „The House of Harmony," the other „Association for harmonious education."

When I asked my friend Anion, he said, „Johannes, Frater Giovanni exerts his negative influence wherever there are people in high places who are interested in subliminal esoteric things.

„Was he a member of all orders?" I queried.

„Yes," Anion countered. "During one of my encounters with Giovanni, he told me that there are religious orders that work with methods, analogous to the Fraternitas Saturni[11], that is, with the power of sexual magic rites. However, all that is just weak compared to the rituals the secret orders and lodges apply. Orders such as the Fraternitas Saturni, OTO, or Golden Dawn constitutes a more public order that merely dabbles in magic. Then, he attempted to make these orders palatable to me, but

---

[11] *See: Gregorius, Gregor. Sexual Magic.*

since all of them are quite useless to me, I declined membership.“

Grandmasters of individual secret lodges maintain contact with each other either through the magic mirror or locales in the part of the astral world that mirrors a

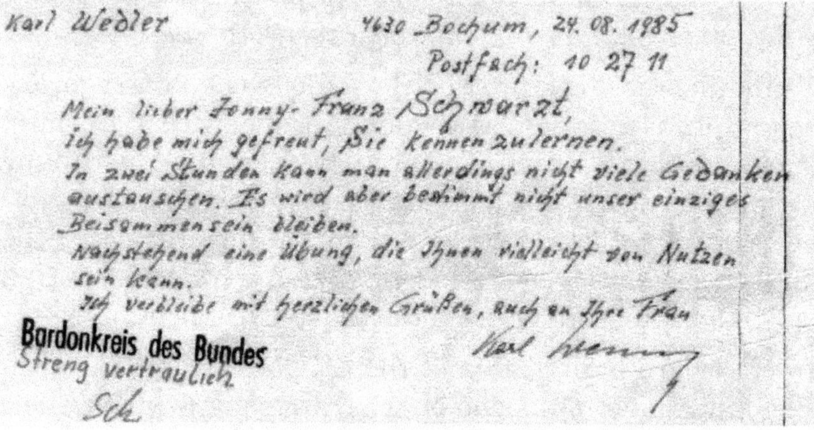

Letter by Giovanni (Wedler) to Anion (Jonny Schwarzt)

I was delighted to have made your acquaintance. Alas, within two hours, we could not exchange many ideas. Surely, this will not be the only time we will get together. Attached are instructions for some exercises that you might find useful. Best wishes to you and also to your wife,
Karl Wedler

physical location where they assemble. One may compare these gathering locales to a peak designated Blocksberg (or Brocken), which is located in the Harz Mountains (Saxony-Anhalt in Eastern Germany), where witches gather in the astral mirror of the peak. Hitler, who, aside from his mediumistic talent, was ignorant of all the occult activities of these lodges and orders, and hat no practical abilities. His fixation rested upon world domination. As the Führer, he wanted to be worshipped like a God, a supreme being that is superior to all others. In a way, Fraternitas Saturni shares a similar view, where members presume that they are superior to Saturn, superior to fate. Hitler, being a true megalomaniac, desired to close or destroy all lodges and also orders, including the FOGC, to exercise world domination freely. Albeit owed to his ignorance and his inability, he sought the assistance of Franz Bardon, who was familiar with all lodges and orders. Bardon fearlessly denied Hitler and only hinted that the symbol and underlying concept of the swastika are angled, and hence it will topple. Bardon's prediction was correct.

During the war, Hitler only launched attacks when they were astrologically favorable. Moreover, he waited until the stars and planets posed an advantageous constella-

Blocksberg (also called Brocken (Engl. boulder) peak, where the witches gather.

tion. It would have been an easy feat for a black magician to influence the course of the war through magical means, but their demon masters had other plans. These magicians would have died a horrible death, had they acted averse to the will of their masters. The life and death of Urbain Grandier should serve as a stern example. First, the torturers crushed Grandier's legs to a pulp, and then the executioners hoisted Grandier up on the center pole of the stake. Grandier was held upright with an iron hoop. After the fire was lit, a compassioned henchman attempted to strangle Grandier, but the fire grew too intense. A re-

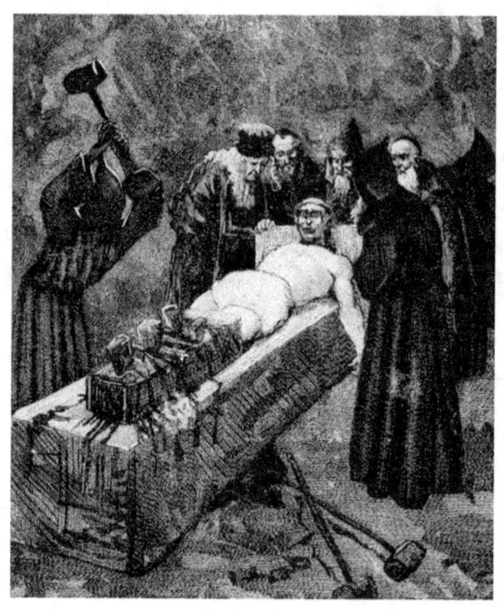

Torture of Grandier with the "Boot." (Source: mindspaceapocalypse. wordpress.com)

port states that Grandier attempted in vain to strangle himself and consequently burned to death.

Some authors state that black magic orders use human sacrifices to aid their incantations. There exist gruesome techniques of invoking negative genii that involve human and/or animal sacrifice. Various sexual-magical orders were founded, in which demons were conjured by utilizing such inhumane practices. Naturally, karma will eventually demand retribution by those magic practitioners, as noted in the paragraph above. A horrific death constitutes only the beginning of torment, these individuals will have to endure.

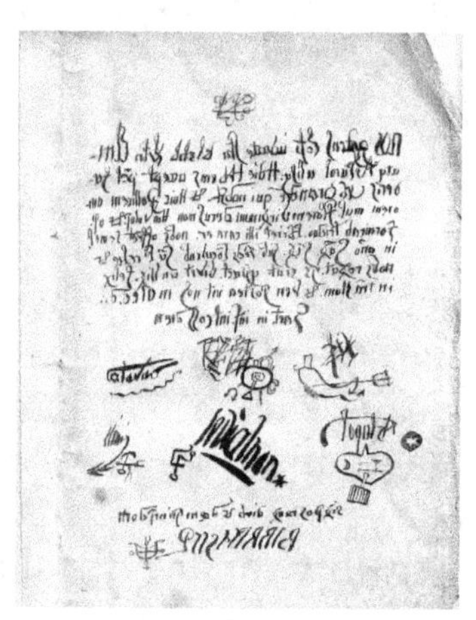

A written pact by Urban Grandier

6.
Hitler's Alleged Occult Abilities

Aside from his mediumistic ability, Hitler never possessed occult power at any time of his life. Nevertheless, he was capable of astounding feats, which, at times, exceeded the limits of the humanly possible. A reason for his sheer super-human characteristics at times is found in the realm of the occult, although he was not directly responsible for causing the preceding effects.

The following lists Hitler's true abilities:

A report states that the Führer had seven very young girlfriends during his Viennese days.

Six of them committed suicide, and one ended up in a psychiatric institution. There are claims that Hitler performed sexual magic to use the charge created to conjure demonic entities. However, the most plausible argument favors Hitler having these young girls vampirized, and consequently depleting their life force. He then utilized these charges for his visions.

Hitler's girlfriend, Eva Braun, wrote in a letter that he needed her only, for one thing, gives rise to suspicions that he had abused her for sexual magic purposes as well.

Heinrich Himmler needed Hitler and Eva Braun for a Black Mass when specific causes were produced to utilize for the ascension of Hitler as the Führer by charging the secretions with ideas to be realized. Hitler had no children with Eva Braun because he saw himself as the father of the nation. He considered his sexuality for other purposes than procreation.

Hitler purportedly possessed a photographic memory. He demonstrated this ability by producing the most precise drawings from memory, quote lengthy excerpts from newspapers. Professor Theodor Gissinger, a master naturalist, recalls Hitler's eccentricity when Hitler had lively dialogues with wind-swept trees. Being a perpetual night owl, Hitler embarked on lengthy, lonely walks in the forest at night for indulging in his visions and tasks of the future.

Hitler checked out of the men's boardinghouse on the summer solstice. The timing was decidedly curious, but it seems that no one is certain whether he became a member of the FOGC or not. However, witnesses state that Hitler left the men's boardinghouse on 21.6.1910 for three days. It is presumed that he did attend the infamous drawing of the death ticket. It is unlikely that Hitler, who at the time appeared like a penniless vagrant, had been a member of the FOGC. Had it been the case, the Fraters would have supported him immediately with financial means to establish himself in society. Hitler's sister, Paula, said that her brother possessed a powerful internal radiance that was endowed to him by higher powers. She did have some rudimentary knowledge of the higher powers that stood behind her brother. He had a radiant aura and a certain charisma that drove women into sexual ecstasy. This electrifying charisma drew the masses to follow and worship him. Neither before nor after him had there been a leader who has enchanted the masses the way he did.

Not surprisingly, Hitler's favorite colors were black, red (Mars), and brown (Earth), which advanced hermetic adepts consider to be hell. That I indeed a bizarre and morbid mixture of colors.

Heinz Linge, Hitler's chief of personal service, accompanied and served his fellow countryman for ten years, wrote a book about the Führer. The latter reports that the bunker of the Wolfsschanze[12] headquarter roughly resembled a pyramid and that Hitler felt transferred to Egypt as a result. Since he could not construct such a mental atmosphere alone, he had to utilize more material forms to create such an atmosphere. Any true adept would have done so quickly. Linge further reports, that Hitler's physical health has sharply deteriorated by 1945, but his photographic memory and mental energy remained incredible. The being behind Hitler endowed him with such mental prowess to exploit Hitler for its purposes to ultimately abandon him in the end. To illustrate the pow-

Wolfsschanze (Wolf's Lair), Hitler's command HQ in Poland then and now

er of this being, Linge further states that Hitler usually precisely sensed what everyone around him was thinking. For example, a guest sitting at the communal table cringed when he heard Hitler immediately take a guest's yet unexpressed objections or views and destroyed and objections during many of his famous tantrums.

As adverted to before, Hitler could only achieve this feat through the assistance of counter-genii (negative princi-

---

[12] *Wolfsschanze (Eng. Wolf's Lair) was one of Hitler's Command Headquarters during WW II. Hitler used the term „Wolf" frequently since the name Adolf connotes wolf.*

pals). One being sought out Hitler because Hitler's predisposition and interest served the being on its mission. Hitler embodied the negative principle on a broad spectrum. Before his infamous speeches, Hitler's personal demon Godhead entered the Führer's body to exert a better influence over the speech audiences. Although Hitler was quite circumspect about this process, he did not receive proper occult training to act on his own without this Godhead. After all, Hitler was merely a prenatally trained medium and instrument for the negative side.

Sometimes a mighty negative Deity will intervene decisively in the fate of humankind because no single human being could bear such an amassment of negative karma. Positive beings also assert earthly influence, such as the chief principal Asamarc, who had taken over a mission in ancient Egypt, or the principal of dreams – Nahum – who wrote *The Book of Nahum*, which constitutes the seventh of the twelve books of the prophets in the *Old Testament*.

Hitler's situation was somewhat different. Since he had been destined to rise and become the absolute leader of the German people, Goebbels, Himmler, and Göring arranged a mediumistic evocation, in which the Mars-God Samuel obsessed Hitler. Whenever he had needed certain occult powers, he called upon this God, so that the Führer could act like a God (the power of a God).

My friend Ariane had seen an exciting show on television. Hitler stood in front of a kiosk, small, hunched and inconspicuous, and wretched. Suddenly a light emanated, above and behind him, which, upon entering him, immediately propped him up, and he began to speak in his usual dynamic tone. The masses were thrilled again by his speeches. A commentator of the show mentioned that it seemed as if a higher being, unbeknownst to Hitler, had entered his body. The Führer was possessed by this being and began adapting counter-genius' characteristics. Only in this way could he exert an extreme influence over the German people and motivate and fascinate the masses into carrying out his will.

Hitler always withdrew when he was drafting his plans since the demon wanted to contact him intuitively to accord instructions. The possessive condition made Hitler feel powerful and more infatuated with absolute domination. Hitler's quote *I am convinced that nothing will happen to me because I gather that Providence has destined me for my work"*, was intuitively conveyed by this counter-genius. Even before Hitler came to power, he already lost his humanity and took on the characteristics of a demon. These traits allowed Hitler to realize that he no could no longer become a genuine human again. In Pictures and portraits of Hitler, one can see an almost non-human, demonic expression in his eyes. The demon genius deliberately transformed and conditioned Hitler through negative astral and mental vibrations. Although, as adverted to before, Hitler had become circumspect of this change and allowed it to happen in exchange for the power that Hitler later exerted over the German people and the nations that he subjugated. He desired to become the sole ruler of the planet and titled himself the coming ruler of the world.

August Kubizek, Hitler's childhood friend, mentions that Hitler could lose himself in a state of ecstasy and become enraptured entirely as if a different being was speaking through him.

Over the years, his voice, facial expression, and content of his words seemed to have evolved. He no longer spoke of wanting to become an artist, but also wished to become a tribune of the people; he had a mission to consummate.

Through to the protection of his demon, Hitler never had taken security precautions when in public and offered an easy target for an assassin at his massive pompous rallies. He stated: „*I know that I will not die before the historical task, for which Providence has destined me, will be fulfilled. I will never die at the hands of others.*" This statement of self- assuredness demonstrates his nature and his reliance upon this counter-genius.

The following are a few examples of botched attempts on Hitler's life: Bottles of brandy, filled with explosives, were deposited in the Führer airplane to bring down his plane. A special train deliberately was laced with explosives without going off; the assassins' bombs were discovered prematurely or failed to explode. Although assassins accepted their deaths in suicide attacks, none proved successful. A sniper missed him from a distance of two meters (6.5 feet); Hitler was poisoned, without results. These are numerous little-known attempts on his life. The best-known assassination attempt was the failed July 20 plot, masterminded by Claus von Stauffenberg, who placed a bomb at the Führer's Wolfsschanze. Hitler survived because one of his doubles was present in the room when the explosion occurred.

Were all assassination failure circumstantial and coincidental? Franz Bardon states in *The Practice of Magical Evocation*, in the chapter *Advantages and Disadvantages of Evocation Magic*: „*If the sorcerer has evoked an indifferent and less active being and if the sorcerer's desire, if it were realised, would not harm him, it might, now and then, give a token of sympathy and do what the sorcerer wants done…. Should a sorcerer or necromancer succeed in actually calling the head of a certain sphere into the physical world by the ecstatic elevation of his spirit, such a head, if it is a negative one, will always try to get under his influence not only the soul but also the spirit of the sorcerer in order to make him fully dependent. The sorcerer usually realizes during his second or third operation that he is no longer able to get himself into the same state of ecstasy which previously helped him to have a certain influence on the concerned sphere."*

Deliberating what he has achieved at the zenith of achievements, Hitler said: *"This has not been merely one man's effort alone. "*

This statement is an allusion to the counter-genius and the being's support. Hitler compares hatred as a permanent and unchangeable, as steel. To him, hate is an expression of human passion that stands above all scientific cognition.

Hitler survived all attempts, not because of the incompetence of his assassins, but owed to an uninterrupted sequence of improbabilities, as there were forty-two documented assassination attempts on Hitler's life. W. Berthold delineated these attempts in detail in his book *The 42 Assassinations on Adolf Hitler.*

*

Unlike his comrades during World War I, Hitler never went drinking during front leaves, never went to brothels, or indulged in other amusements. He lay quietly and silently on his cot and indulged in pipe dreams, to reach for the pie in the sky. He had plenty of opportunities during battle lulls. In battle, he never displayed any fear resulting from the guidance of a demon.

A front-line private's report states: As unbelievable as it may sound, Hitler urged me to jump forward, and a moment later, a hissing hot projectile hit the ground behind me and exploded. My nerves had failed me. I did not want to move, and I sank into an unbearable abyss of apathy. Then, Hitler would speak kind words of encouragement and give me hope. He said that one day all our heroism would be rewarded a thousand times over by the homeland. So my comrade lifted me out of my depression and sinking hopelessness. Soon, we jumped out of our trenches and dashed though no-man's-land to attack the enemy, and again, we returned hours later unscathed in one piece.

John Keegan states in his book, *The Mask of the Command*, that *"Hitler remained unharmed throughout all battles and earned the title "the invulnerable. "He fought in forty-eight battles and survived four and a half years of the most bloody battles, in which the chance of survival was sometimes less than 10%. The longer the war dragged on, the more sensational Hitler's survival had become. "*

His foreboding of the front lines left an uncanny impression. Following his initial inner demonic voice, he dashed to safety from a spot that was hit by a grenade moments later that killed those who did not follow Hitler to safety.

Hitler wrote the following poem that, according to Ariane, was inspired by a superior counter-genius.

"Sometimes during rough nights,
I approach Wotan's oak in the silent grove,
The one with dark powers a covenant to lichen.
The runes in the moonlight conjure me,
And all who enjoyed the day.
They are stunted by a magic formula
They are filled with apathy – but instead of
braiding a wreath,
They solidify into stalagmite rock.
I separate this way, all unbidden from appointed ones.
I reach into the wellspring of all fibulae,
And bestow to the noble and righteous,
My formulae of blessings and prosperity."

When Hitler returned from the war in 1919, he had a satori experience, a sudden bout of enlightenment that would guide him to the zenith, a megalomaniacal leader, and a prophet of the German people. Hitler interpreted his war blindness as a myth of revival. He believed that he was called by Providence to consummate his mission on earth. Blindness was not unusual, for many became temporarily blinded by poisonous gas, but eventually regained their full sight. However, Hitler interpreted his blindness as a calling by none less than Divine Providence.

Hitler (left) as a soldier during WWI.

The Swiss psychologist and mystic, Carl Gustaf Jung, mentioned in 1919 that something threatening, even catastrophic loomed on the horizon. Hitler entered the stage with piercing eyes and invincible confidence. He possessed a fascinating air of superiority and radiated an iron will that brought the masses to their knees in awe of their Führer's presence. All the while, Hitler's charge of vitality and charisma that aided his plan of dominion came from his counter-genius. This power gave Hitler the upper hand over rank and file. He was a "godlike" human.

Hitler's former superior officer stated that *I do not recognize Hitler anymore. There is an unknown fire that burns within him. The way he ecstatically delivered his words and the way he stares during his speeches, I have never seen anything like it. Sweat ran down his face; it is quite incredible.*" The effects of his speeches were uncommon. He was a perfect actor who mastered his role brilliantly. He spoke intuitively with his mission in mind and thus struck the core of the people. He remained to be an artist, a leader who mastered the art of manipulation. Hitler's canvas was now the masses that he led.

"The Austrian-British philosopher, Ludwig Wittgenstein, was known for his charisma, and the striking expression of his eyes," Harald Strohm stated. *"He not only succeeded in hypnotizing his students. Even eminent professors fell under his spell; even when they did not understand or rejected his thoughts. Rudolf Carnap, a German language philosopher, compared him to a biblical prophet or seer. John Maynard Keynes wrote about Wittgenstein's arrival at Cambridge station in the earnest irony: 'God has arrived. I met him on the five-fifteen train.' And Moritz Schlick's wife reported on her husband's feelings he expressed when he set out to meet Wittgenstein: 'It was as if he were going on a pilgrimage,' she said, 'and he told me that Wittgenstein was one of the greatest geniuses.'"*

In his speeches in 1923, Hitler mentioned several times that his role model the Roman dictator Lucius Cornelius Sulla. According to the historian Helmut Berve, *"Sulla was an uncanny man without human emotions and empathy who felt he was "an instrument of a higher, callous will. The Roman dictator proved to be an ethical nihilist, cruel monster, filled with unlimited vindictiveness, and a cynical, shuddering coldness of heart, capable at most of a sentimental softness like many a violent nature."* Those are all the character traits that Hitler shared with the Roman emperor (sociopathy).

Hitler compared himself in private circles with the Messiah, who chased the rabble out of the temple. His character proved decisive for his mission. Hitler was calculating, diabolically cunning, devious, insincere, hypocritical, a dazzling deceiver, and mendacious. For his mission of becoming an absolute ruler, these character traits served him well, as did his passion for destruction. In his speeches, Adolf Hitler repeatedly invoked the idea that Divine Providence, bestowed the mission of creating the superhuman "Aryan" and accelerate evolution. He viewed himself to be the creator of a new world, a world master, and redeemer. Goebbels viewed Hitler was a "fallen angel," an allusion to Hitler's completely exaggerated veneration and glorification of the Biblical fall of Lucifer.

Hitler directed his attention only to what he found useful and advantageous for his task ahead to consummate his mission.

All else was of no interest to him. While attending Wagner's opera, *The Ring of the Nibelungen,* Hitler fell into an ecstatic state outside himself as he did during his speeches. Kubizek reported that a demonic presence affected his consciousness to an extreme so he would ignore everything around him. He became restless and energetically charged.

All subordinates who worked with Hitler for a long time became extremely servile over time (cf. Satan, the seducer). Everyone feared his demonic tantrums. All the officers and ministers were terrified of him. Although he had been of average physical height and statue, everyone feared Hitler's wrath and paralyzing anger.

Once a human being interacts with a dominant demon being, he transforms partly into that being. Such a person acts as a deputy of that being in the physical realm.

All the negative traits that the being possesses will be projected. The result is hating, destruction, enslavement, and suffering.

Hitler stood, with locked knees, a rigidly erect body, and a motionless face, at the Nuremberg party congresses for 4 to 5 hours and displayed the gesture of victory and healing with his right hand outstretched (the "Heil Hitler greeting" is identical to the Ka-Rune position). The power present in the Ka-Rune gave Hitler strength and invincibility. However, one has to deliberate that if the forces of the runes are used destructively, they will eventually turn against the rune practitioner. This rune practice will show now result for the ordinary person, but Hitler's partisanship with a high-ranked counter-genius allowed him to enjoy practical results.

Ernst Hanfstaengl, a German-American politician businessman and financial supporter of Hitler, was convinced that owed to Hitler's peculiar behavior, no one ever knew

"Hitlergruß," the KA-Rune gesture

with absolute certainty what his intentions were. Hanfstaengl wrote about Hitler's unparalleled ability to hoard secrets, and no one learned more than what one had in a particular situation. No one was exempt, not even his future wife, Eva Braun. For this reason, his perpetual secrecy, Hitler was a true enigma, even in his closest circles. A hermetic knows that real power is in silence; i.e., one's mission will not be compromised. He used everyone for his performances and his mission. He had accomplished nothing; he just used everything he found in his name. Human, all too human does not exist with him. Individuals associated with Hitler were convinced that no one will ever unravel Adolf Hitler's real persona because he had so many of them. He had attained the mastery deception.

A claim states that Hitler's movement would make Hitler and German state the master race of earth. Hitler viewed himself as worthy of being a substitute for God.

Since the beginning of his ascent to power, Hitler intended for Germany to subjugate Europe. Consequently, Europe would dominate the world with one world ruler at the helm of power, and he could achieve this goal only through war. Hitler had even drawn plans which connected Europe and Russia — as far as deep into Mongolia — with roads. One of Hitler's quotes confirms this statement: *"The patches of small states that still exist in Europe today must be liquidated. Our goal is to create a united Europe. "*

Many of Hitler's quotations conjure parallels to satanic philosophy through statements such as *"I will lead all people back to God, but by force,"* or *"My pedagogy is hard. The weak must be chiseled away. Germany's youth will grow up in my order's castles and will terrify the world. I want a violent, domineering, intrepid, cruel youth. They must endure pain and be without feebleness and tenderness. They will become magnificent beasts of prey and seek their prey with their steely, beastly eyes.*

"Hitler, however, was averse pain and had his physician dull any painful malady or injury with potent medications. Hitler's dentist had to fully anesthetize the "fearless" Führer to perform even simple dental work. His words about Germany's youth enduring pain did not truly reflect ahis low threshold of pain.

Another of Hitler's quotes reveals his reason for wars: Wars are not fought to defeat nations, but to create a state. Intuitively, he proved to be right.

The "National Socialist Movement," one of the largest Neo-Nazi groups in the USA during a demonstration in Washington D.C.

Individuals who exert influence on the course of politics are mostly backers and advisors of top politicians and work in the background. These influencers utilize their occult abilities, e.g., by shifting consciousness and thus influencing the mind through their superior will. An essay in the occult magazine *Der eigene Weg* (The Individual Path), published by the runologist Friedrich B. Marby, delineates this phenomenon of shifting consciousness. There are situations in which these influencers and mental manipulators associate with many well-known esteemed people socially on whom they exert their influence. These individuals will pass on an implanted order to others like a contagion. Anion justified this statement with the assertion that politicians in high offices spend much time in their profession, often conducting negotiations for hours on end, and deep into the night and have no time for lengthy and rigorous spiritual training. They have no time to withdraw for five minutes for exercises. Hence, politicians are merely the instruments of the truly powerful.

The spiritual realm determines all actions, a fact that denotes that Hitler did not continue to inspire racial hatred and national pride after his death. The counter-genius that guided Hitler continues to work in the astral realm, unrecognized and in secret. There are still many discussions about Hitler, and he still haunts the consciousness of many. Hitler had become an unforgettable phenomenon. Many yearn for a return of Hitler and his institution. Countless Neo-Nazi and white supremacy groups celebrate Hitler and National Socialism. It the USA, the First Amendment allows Nazi materials to be printed, and public display of Nazi paraphernalia and Neo-Nazi groups openly spread their racist messages. The beings of the negative astral realm have placed causes into the material world through. The Akasha chronicles preserve all concepts and ideas of the Third Reich, and some individuals are tuned into these ideas and realizing these causes, long after Hitler's passing.

The physician Dr. Georg Lomer who was also an Ariosoph and occultist, castigated the shape and color of the German Nazi flag. He stated the swastika symbol, a holy symbol, should be golden on a blue background to express its true dignity and distinction. For the swastika embodies the sun and represents the Aryan (noble) God-human. Black on a red background are the colors of

The political Swastika flag was used troughout the Third Reich

the negative war planet Mars and does not represent a human-divine symbol.

In the German occult magazine *Die andere Welt* (The Other World), appeared an article that supports the statement that Hitler was in contact with a demon.

We Saw Hitler's Demon

by

Hermann Medinger (Vienna)

"At last, the hour of Hitler's invasion, so eagerly awaited by many Austrians, was approaching, and the end to this general political stagnation has approached.

On that day in March, when the Führer paraded through Vienna, I was the guest of a family who had an apartment on the Viennese Opernring from which we follow to see the entire show. We were a small group of guests, consisting of prominent industrialists, artists, and lawyers with their ladies, including my wife and myself. Gourmet canapés and exquisite wines were available at a richly adorned buffet.

Suddenly we heard loud, enthusiastic shrieks echoing from the Ringstrasse. As we took our window seats, we noted Hitler below, standing in his car, gliding past us like a God-sent man, accompanied by the music of the Grail motif of Richard Wagner's 'Lohengrin.' People acted like maniacs. Crying hysterically, screaming, women fell into hysterical convulsions, children lost their way and wandered around crying. In a word: It was the typical scene of mass hysteria and ecstasy that the appearance of false prophets triggers.

Hitler standing in his Mercedes convertible.

Our small party, watching Hitler's appearance from the noble salon of a downtown condominium, was emotionally moved and exalted. Every guest stared out the window in awe of the spectacle down in the streets.

A loud burst of broken glass in the room jolted us out of our trance. We all turned around simultaneously and saw my wife standing at the table, trembling. The wine glass that she held had slipped out of her hands and shattered on the floor. She appeared anxious and glanced at the window with frightened eyes. Her hands trembled, and she slowly opened her mouth to speak. After a short pause, she uttered with a shaky voice: "Why are you rejoicing, you all have no reason for it. Hitler will bring us grief and destruction. He is possessed by demons."

General dismay and outrage gripped our party. Then I looked closely at the Führer down below and noticed dark shadows wavering around Hitler. It seemed as if black tatters, like fluttering groups bats escaping a cave at dusk, surrounded Hitler. Another lady from our society observed this phenomenon and confirmed my perception. All others, however, were deceived by this false prophet, looking at him favorably until the 1000-Year Reich collapsed around them.

Hitler hat a quite innocent-looking face as a youth. He failed at school – and yet this rose to such power. His speeches were not the speeches of a mere man. Hitler's former art teacher Otto Abetz said that Hitler was a combination of Jeanne D'Arc and Charlie Chaplin. Like a saint, he heard voices, and then he could achieve great things. He kept talking about Providence having commissioned him to bring Judgement upon mankind. What madness.“

At the end of his life, Hitler, struck by Parkinson's disease and the onset of dementia, was reduced to a hunched, nervous, trembling old man, although he was only 56 years of age. Hitler's astral elements shifted because of constant contact with the demon, and had to resort to heavy drugs to compensate for his elemental imbalance. Dr. Theo Morell, Hitler's personal physician, propped Hitler up with a cocktail of dangerous drugs. All these years, Hitler spent communicating with a high ranked demon, depleted the life force from his body and soul. One can see his trembling hand in one of the last film footage. An individual who is untrained in the occult arts cannot extract the necessary forces from the universe and must resort to using his life force. Once this demonic being abandoned him, Hitler became a shell of his former self. His fears exacerbated and turned into panic, anxiety, pathological paranoia, and suicidal intentions. He lost the ability to withstand the cosmic vibrations, as Bardon states in his second work, *The Practice of Magical Evocation.*

An additional reason for Hitler's downfall poses the circumstance that Franz Bardon interfered with Hitler's mission. Divine Providence did not authorize Bardon to kill Hitler owed to karmic reasons but permitted Bardon to make life more difficult for the Führer.

A scene in the novel *Frabato* delineates the Grandmaster of the FOGC in Dresden writing to a high government official to destroy Bardon through conventional means. Contrary to the assumption of some readers, this person was not Adolf Hitler, but an eminently influential member of the Templars.

A quote from the Hitler biographer, Hermann Rauschning, states that *"Hitler had conditions that approached a state of paranoia and a dissociative identity disorder. He often woke up at night and wandered around restlessly. All lights were switched on. At times, Hitler gathered young people around him to have company during the hours of manifest horror with him. These afflictions transformed Hitler's personality, and he displayed a quite malignant character. Someone told me that Hitler woke up at night with convulsions. He cried out for help or sat frozen and motionless on the edge of his bed. Then, fear would make him tremble intensely enough to rattle the entire bed. Then, he would utter incomprehensible words and gasp for air as if he suffocated. He would stand in the room, looking around with frightened eyes and scream 'He, ...he has been here.' His lips turned blue. Sweat would drip down his face. Suddenly he would recite numbers. Hitler would ramble incoherent words and phrases like a madman. It sounded horrible. He would compose words, entirely strangely articulating words. Then, he would stand completely still again while moving his lips. An assistant would wipe the sweat of Hitler's face, and he had been given something to drink. Then, he would shout out: 'There, there! Look! Look in the corner. Who's there?' He had stomped his feet, screamed. He had been convinced that this was nothing unusual in his room, and then he would gradually calm down. Then, he would sleep for many hours. Once awake, he would be pleasant for a while." There are many similar reports about Hitler's strange nocturnal behavior. Hitler's terrible nightmares and hallucinations are caused by Franz Bardon and a principal being he had sent to stir Hitler's emotions and fears.*

7.
Aryan Philosophy

All Ariosophical concepts, i.e., rites, evocation methods, and exercises, originated from Master Arion. The name Arion – Ario-sophy – connotes nobility and wisdom of the divine light. Thus, Aryan attributes are virtuousness and kindness.

The Aryans of the ancient times were true leaders of the early people. Because of their high spiritual rank those, individuals are the true lords and guides of humankind. Their dominion on earth spanned the mineral, plant, animal, and human realm and sat at the right hand of God. Their motives were pure and noble. Their hair was blond, like the sun at noon. Their blue eyes symbolized to the astral plane, which represents the number ten. Ten is the perfect number. The "race" of the Aryans originally descended from the Atlantean race and have the mission, the Magnum Opus, to transmit their highest wisdom to others, not by force, but with love and insight.

Like Christianity, the Aryan philosophy includes a divine trinity. However, the trinity of Aryan philosophy represents the three planes and bodies: The first God is Wotan, who represents the mental realm and body, the spirit, and the beginning. Hönir dominion and sphere of influence is the astral realm and astral body. Thus, he represents the Divinity of the soul and the middle. The Godhead Loki reigns over the material realm and the physical body and represents the end. As the Lord of the Earth, he constitutes absolute dominion over everything physical.

According to Dr. Georg Lomer and other Ariosophical philosophers, Balder is analogous to Christ, and his brother, Loki, is Lucifer. The German artist Fidus figuratively represented as Lucifer in one of his drawings. The Relationship between Balder-Christ and Loki-Lucifer illustrates the spiritual fact that positive and negative forces collaborate harmoniously for the development of the human race. This collaboration can be interpreted as a loving relationship between two opposite currents. Hinduism represents this relationship of high and low, or passive, and active in the marriage of Shiva and Shakti, and Daoism utilizes the symbol of Yin and Yang – heaven and earth (positive and negative). This relationship is also analogous to the relationship of the micro- and macrocosm, and the Minor and Major Arcana. Thus, the Aryan religion represents a harmonious holistic development of humans towards God, the Allfather, the Father.

Loki-Lucifer portrait by Fidus (Hugo Höppener)

All three above mentioned deities are presented to us as *Kunnig, Rammar,* and *Roskr* (wise, powerful, and bold), which, in turn, is analog to the three colors of the planes – blue, white and gold. Gold, the color of the sun, already directs to the sun cult, which the ancient Teutons cultivated. In a sun cult, the sun is the giver of life, a promoter of fertility, salvation, and healing. Figuratively, the sun was represented by a spoked wheel, a sun wheel with either with six or eight spokes. The number of wheel spokes depended on the way this wheel symbol was used quabbalistically. The sun deity then merged with the Roman God Jupiter, whose name means heaven or sky. The original idea of a sun chariot and horse further deepens this observation. Apollo presents the sun and light and purity, but also poetry, art, and music (sun, and Jupiter) in Greek mythology.

Counterclockwise – Negative; Clockwise – Positive

Later, the Gnostics exploited universal laws for egocentric, personal gains, and distorted them of vile benefits. Ultimately, they directed their central attention to the left-turning sun wheel, the counterclockwise turning swastika, a symbol of the Lord of the Earth, whom they worshipped. In the early 20th century, the maxim connoted that "honest work makes an honest man out of a crook." An adage posted at the entrance gates to several concentration camps, including the notorious death camp of Auschwitz Arbeit macht frei" (work makes you free), is a spiritually affirmative maxim that has been perverted by the Nazis Hitler. Its original meaning connotes that work on oneself will advance once spirit; thus, providing more freedom. The Nazis turned the original intent into a mockery. It was meant to mock the new arrivals at the camps. To the Nazis, it meant "work until you die. Then, you are free."

Through mental conditioning, the Nazis saw themselves as God-like master humans who spread their philosophy through violence and tyranny. In an analogous but less tyrannical way, American imperialism uses this maxim of work equating progress and democracy and freedom and forces their brand of Americanism on other nations. Specific lodges consider Saturn, who equates to Satan, as the great educator of humanity. Satan is guardian-of-the-threshold, and to pass, one must prove oneself to continue. The members of these lodges and idealize and worship Saturn as their demiurge. Through the great seducer, many have developed a distorted philosophy and world view.

8.
Ariosophic Socienties

The following occult orders appeared in large quantities in the 20th century. However, most of these societies were of no hermetic value except the groups that Georg Lomer and Friedrich B. Marby founded. This list is supplied only with a few brief comments:

The Guido von List Society

It was founded in Vienna by Guido List. This society had members from the aristocracy, industrialists, and businessmen (in those days, women did not have leading positions in the world of business). The "Sieg Heil "greeting was coined by this society, which Hitler promptly appropriated, like so many other things. The founder of this society published a series of ariosophical books.

ONT – Order of the New Templar

Lanz von Liebenfels founded this order. He was a former Cistercian monk, so he enjoyed a spiritual pre-schooling. His order represented a new foundation of the order of the Temple. Liebenfels published the magazine Ostara, which contained, among other things, topics such as sexual magic. His members were also capitalists and industrialists. The order's seat was in Austria. Liebenfels was a zealous writer of countless works. He wrote about sexual magic in the publication Ostara, Issue *43: Introduction to Sexual Physics or Love as Odic En*ergy. In it, he delineates that everything associated with instinct as an Od energy that emanates from life force. The attraction of two people depends on opposing Od currents, the electric and magnetic currents. Furthermore, he writes that the sexual Od reaches far from its originator and connotes that man and woman are always sexually attracted to each other, even at a distance. A hermetic can work with these forces externally and distant.

Teutonic Order (Germanenorden)

Founded by Hermann Pohl and Theodor Fritsch in Leipzig in 1912. The members allegedly practiced runic magic due to their relations to the Guido-von-List Society. Since the founding members were nationalists, they harbored anti-Semitic sentiments. Their attitude was purely negative and destructive in a spiritual sense.

Teutonic Order Walvater

This order worshipped the Allfather-Wotan (Odin) and published the magazines Runen and Runenforscher (Rune Researcher).

Wehrmanngesellschaft (Defenders' Society)

Published the ariosphical magazine Wehrmann (Defender).

Thule Gesellschaft (Thule Society)

Rudolf von Sebottendorf (Adam Rudolf Glauer) lectured on astrology, numerology, and meditation. This society was supposedly associated with the Teutonic Order. His work on The Practice of Ancient Turkish Freemasonry also lends insight into the magical thinking of the Ariosophical Order. As mentioned earlier, this order was the introductory order from which talented members were selected to join the much more dominant and actively working Nordic Thule Order.

The Edda Society

The founder of this society was the runologist and Edda translator, Rudolf John Gorsleben, who translated the Edda into German and wrote some works with a racist undertone. Friedrich Marby claimed that Gorsleben plagiarized his works. The Edda Society published the two magazines, H*ag All* and A*ryan Freedom*.

Union of the Aryan Invisible

This union was founded by Siegfried A. Kummer, the author of the runic works **Rune Might and Rune Magic** (translated into English by Stephen Flowers). These two works are very symbolic, and Franz Bardon had Rune Magic translated into Czech for his students. Kummer published the magazines **Valhalla** and **Runa**, of which the latter posed as the official magazine of the rune academy Runa. The instructional magazine **Rune Whisper** which reports numerous accounts of rune-practitioner experiences. However, according to Dr. Lomer, these accounts proved to be exaggerated. One must take that the dangerous nature of rune practice taxed Kummer's reasoning. After WW II, Kummer lived as an artist in East Germany, where he received prices for his art. He never practiced the runes again until he died in 1977 Kamenz, former East Germany.

Orion Society and the Union of the Pure

This order is a hermetically oriented society founded by the druid Friedrich B. Marby. He was the only one among the Ariosoph who demonstrated real practical knowledge of rune magic. He published the two magazines *Der eigene Weg* **(The Own Path) and** *Forschung und Erfahrung* **(Research and Skill). Initially,** Marby, the Nazi regime banned him from writing any further books or teaching occult practices. Consequently, he was denounced and arrested in 1938. Marby later spent the next 97 months in protective custody within the concentration camps of Flossenburg and Dachau. American troops liberated him in April of 1945. Although Marby was arrested and imprisoned on the grounds of being an anti-national socialist occultist, Marby possessed true quabbalistic abilities that posed a danger to the regime. Before 1933, Marby published hermetic rune books, the eight volumes called Ru*nenbibliothek* (Rune Library). In reference to his books, Marby stated that the reader always has to read "between the lines" to extract the truth. Marby repeatedly claimed that the Nazi regime and its philosophy had nothing to do with the Aryan movement.

Georg Lomer

Dr. Lomer was an Ariosoph who did not establish an actual order, but a spiritual community, which according to his magazine *Asgard* should practice a "sun exercise" (Man-Rune) on Sunday between 11:00-12:00 noon (Standard Time).

9.
The Nordic Thule Order

The Nordic Thule Order is not associated with the FOGC. The name of this order indicates that this order is of Nordic origin. Its members are Thule masters, namely, masters of the Creator Word. Henceforth, the Thule Order is superior to the FOGC, as each Thule member is a master adept; however, this order works with black magic as well. There are several Thule branches in Germany and other countries. Every region has a branch, and Italy hosts quite a few of these branches. The reason is that Italy's government has many corrupt officials; the Vatican is located in the heart of the Italian capital, and organizations such as the Mafia or Camorra thrives. Additionally, the Italians are generally very religious people.

In a documentary about the Mafia, a public prosecutor, placed under the strictest surveillance, was asked why the Mafia cannot be crushed. He replied that it was very well organized and that it was protected by politically influential societies such as *the Order Propaganda Due (P2)*. This prosecutor was asked if these crime syndicates could be toppled. The public prosecutor frowned at the question and stated that there are some secret societies, whereto only a few selected personalities have access. Money or social status plays no role in becoming a member. These orders are closed to ordinary individuals, wealthy or not. Italy has a long history of political instability and mismanagement, and these secret societies influence political parties and politicians

Although one may speculate that the Thule Order vanished during the collapse of the Third Reich, the Thule Order still exists today. When asked, Anion stated the following: *When asked, Anion stated the following: Yes, the order still exists; the order acts unnoticed in secret. Only the outer components of the order, the Thule Society and others connected with it vanished. The order is supervised and dominated by demon principals and constitutes the material antithesis of the spiritual world. Like the Brotherhood of Light, the Thule Order consists twelve masters. These twelve are true* masters and practice evocational magic."

Each one of the Brothers of Light is quite capable of destroying all black magical orders instantly. But they must also abide to universal laws, and evolution. A true adept is able to intervene and exert his influence without being seen or recognized. In principle, they utilize the same magical rituals as the FOGC; however, their admission rites are not adopted from the Freemasons, but are of Nordic origin. For this reason, the Thule members also practice the destructive aspect of demonic rune magic, while they work with spirit beings. Even the Fraterintas Saturni liaised contact to the Thule Order to some of its own members, since the FS origin is also Nordic.

Many believe that Baron von Sebottendorf, a self-assigned nobleman, was master of the elements and the fluids, and some of Hitler's acquaintances were members of this Thule Order. Rudolf Heß who has spent more than half of his life in Spandau prison, did not dare reveal any facts because not even the thickest prison walls would not be able to give sanctuary. It is speculated that individuals who knew the secrets behind the political activities feared horrible retribution by the order and its counter-genii and instead chose the henchmen or rot in prison. Although Dr. Adolf Hemberger, was supported by the German Research Foundation (DFG) in Bad Godesberg (near Bonn, Germany), and other professors of various universities, he dedicated only six pages to the Nordic-Aryan lodges in his writings about the different organizations and federation.

10.
The False Prophets

In the past, a few clairvoyants gave the most exact predictions. As an example of clear prophecies is the book *War Prophecies* by Hans Bender, which proved in detail that the statements are 99% correct in it are not falsified. This book cites letters written in 1914 that describe the exact course of events and timeline of the First and partly of the Second World War.

Alas, many supernatural images, visions, or revelations are produced by swindlers and imposters who only seek financial gratification or admiration by their peers. The known psychic Erik Jan Hanussen dates the presumed demise in his novel *The Fall of New York* at 2320. In reverse, the date would be 2023, which was the date given to the members of the Bardon Circle of the Covenant (Bardonkreis des Bundes) when the Third World War would break out. However, this date does not correspond with future events taking place. There will be no nuclear war since nations, that possess a nuclear weapon arsenal, realize that a nuclear war would prove suicidal. The Austrian occultist Karl Brandler-Pracht and other astrologers have already calculated the imminent collapse and even a world flood. All these speculations that err on the side of reality. Speculations cite that some lodges and orders made necessary preparations, but ultimately, Divine Providence is the absolute authority that acts through the Blue Monks.

Allegedly, new nuclear weapons were developed, whose radioactive fallout is minimized to avoid global contamination. France is supposedly testing such weapons of mass destruction on one of its French archipelago, the

Mururoa Atoll. All those speculations are nonsense since there is no such thing as a "clean" weapon of mass destruction.

Numerous seers and clairvoyants pertinaciously cling to visions of a global nuclear war in the future. Many were influenced by the statements the US Freemason Albert Pike, who allegedly wrote in a letter to the Italian nationalist, politician, and activist Giuseppe Mazzini. In it were detailed events of a Luciferian Plan" that called for the three major world wars. The claim that these letters were ever written came from author Wilhelm G. Carr, whose only source for this document is again a book by Cardinal Caro Rodriguez, a man of the cloth who passionately detested Freemasonry. Allegedly, the Cardinal claims to have seen this infamous letter in the British Library in 1925. However, there is no evidence to support the above claims, and the British Library confirmed that there had never been such a letter in its excellently documented collection. No such letter was exhibited in 1925.

Many rumors and false facts surround the persona of Pike. Supposedly, he was a co-founder of the racist Ku Klux Klan or that he committed atrocities as a Confederate officer during the US civil war. Rumors also claim that he was a Satanist who worshipped Lucifer as the genuine Saviour. No, none of these statements were proven and ultimately turned out to be empty allegations. Léo Taxil, a French journalist who despised Catholicism and Freemasonry, deliberately created many of the rumors that rank around Pike. Taxil's charges included an inner circle of the chosen, named the Taxil's allegations included an inner circle of the chosen, called the Satanic Palladium Order. "According to Taxil, this inner circle would also accept women with whom the members would practice ritual sexual rites and worship of demonic Deities. Furthermore, Taxil interviewed a female witness, Diana

Vaughn, who claimed to have been a lover of Albert Pike and a high priestess of the Palladium. But during a press conference, Taxil cynically rescinded his statements.

There are speculations about families who regard themselves to be descendants of the high priests of ancient orders who perform sacrificial blood rituals that would set causes into motion, which would ultimately lead to a Third World War. The sacri

Albert Pike

fices were to be carried out at the exact locale where the mystic Solomon had once resided.

On January 12, 1952, Chief Rabbi Emanuel Rabinovich proclaimed before a special meeting *of the On January 12, 1952, Chief Rabbi* Emanuel Rabinovich declared before a special meeting of the Emergency Council of European Rabbis“ in Budapest:

„The goal for which we have striven so concertedly for three thousand years is at last within our reach, and because its fulfillment is so apparent, it behooves us to increase our efforts and our caution tenfold. I can safely promise you that before ten years have passed, our race will take its rightful place in the world, with every Jew a king and every Gentile a slave.

You remember the success of our propaganda campaign during the 1930's, which aroused anti-American passions in Germany at the same time we were arousing anti-German passions in America, a campaign which culminated in the Second World War. A similar propaganda cam-

paign is now being waged intensively throughout the world. A war fever is being worked up in Russia by an incessant anti-American barrage while a nation-wide anti-Communist scare is sweeping America. This campaign is forcing all the smaller nations to choose between the partnership of Russia or an alliance with the United States. Our most pressing problem at the moment is to inflame the lagging militaristic spirit of the Americans. The failure of the Universal Military Training Act was a great setback to our plans, but we are assured that a suitable measure will be rushed through Congress immediately after the 1952 elections.

The Russians, as well as the Asiatic peoples, are well under control and offer no objections to war, but we must wait to secure the Americans. This we hope to do with the issue of Anti-Semitism, which worked so well in uniting the Americans against Germany. We are counting heavily on reports of anti-Semitic outrages in Russia to whip up indignation in the United States and produce a front of solidarity against the Soviet power. Simultaneously, to demonstrate to Americans the reality of anti-Semitism, we will advance through new sources large sums of money to outspokenly anti-Semitic elements in America to increase their effectiveness, and we shall stage Anti-Semitic outbreaks in several of their largest cities. This will serve the double purpose of exposing reactionary sectors in America, which then can be silenced, and of welding the United States into a devoted anti-Russian unit.

Within five years, this program will achieve its objective, the Third World War, which will surpass in destruction all previous contests. Israeli, of course, will remain neutral, and when both sides are devastated and exhausted, we will arbitrate, sending our Control Commissions into all wrecked countries. This war will end for all time our struggle against the Gentiles."

All these prophecies surely sound horrifying and spread more fear and terror than they contain facts, because none of his prophecies had occurred. Michael Drosnin's book *The Bible Code* states some claims about predictions for another world war. Some Biblical researchers interpret the quabbalistic *Apocalypse of John* (Revelation of John) as a revelation of a Third World War. Furthermore, some propose that the destruction of Babylon through Yahweh will escalate into a Third World War, in which the USA will fight alongside Israel against Russia, and its oppressed allies, the Arabs. The result will be a global annihilation. This last and bloodiest battle of humankind will find its climax in Armageddon. The final remaining nuclear arsenal will be lobbed against the Russian armies. The second coming of the Messiah will occur during the aftermath of a nuclear holocaust. The gates of heaven will open, and the Savior descends to earth to unite humankind and make Jerusalem the seat of a global government.

According to some prophecies, the USA assumes that the Third World War will be fought in Europe like the First and Second World Wars. One can refer to the former US Secretary of Defense Caspar Weinberger, who said: „*The battlefield of the next conventional war will be Europe and not the United States.*"

Besides, *the before-mentioned reasons for another global war, another prediction from 1949 states: Because of the signs already present today, one has to conclude that by resuming the centuries-old struggle for the catholization of the world and by continuing the fight averse to socialism* humankind, we are in great danger of being plunged into a third world catastrophe. "

Meanwhile, militant Islamic groups have declared the so-called Holy War created a constant fear of terrorist attacks globally.

The USA has rehabilitated and saved its economy through world wars twice in this century. Contemplating the vast government deficit and a proposed recession, the possibility of another world war seems plausible. However, there are other non-military means to engage in a conflict that causes just as much misery as would a military conflict. The US military budget is second to none. Why does a powerful country that is not threatened by military power need such a huge military budget, if not for imperialist reasons? NATO expansion to the former Soviet bloc exemplifies such US imperialist ambitions. There is no other reason to expand NATO eastwards since the cold war is over. In fact, NATO's eastward expansion serves to enforce Anglo-American plans for world domination. We've strived to obtain

According to the US conspiracy theorist (Milton) William Cooper's prognosis, a Third World War would have erupted in mid-1996. He took this information from alleged secret papers that he had photographed during his term of office of the US Navy's secret service branch. Obviously, that has not happened and will not occur. Cooper states that according to classified military and governmental plans, one of the three largest American cities, either New York, San Francisco, or Los Angeles, will be destroyed by a nuclear device.

Consequently, extremists from the Middle East will be charged with this act of terror to justify a Third World War. Even The Grandmaster of the Fraternias Saturni, Gregorius, writes that a nuclear war is inevitable.

Countless books contain horrible prophecies, and mostly including the same scenarios. These authors are merely in the business of making money and gaining prestige. Scenarios range from near-total annihilation to being thrust back to the dark ages. Biblical prophecies in the scriptures are often interpreted in a way to illustrate some ultimate war that will lead to a peaceful period of humanity. However, the result is much different, and a golden age will come in the far future. *Remember: Man reasons and God directs.*"

That leaves us with the infamous French physician, astrologer and psychic, Michel Nostradamus. His lines are interpreted and re-interpreted by researchers of this field until Nostradamus' stanzas became useless and confusing. Repeatedly interpreters speak of a looming global nuclear war. Fighting wars is costly, and most countries experience substantial financial deficits. The wars in Iraq and Afghanistan are devouring vast amounts of dollars. How would a major war that would destroy most resources enrich any nation, large or small? The result of the course of the future will prove to be quite different from war and destruction.

One occultist who never claimed to be a clairvoyant was Dr. Georg Lomer. His visions depart from the rest. One of his books is titled *The Coming World Catastrophes.* His prophecies are based on a prophecy found in nature, which lends more meaning to his predictions than any previous prophecies.

Albert Einstein was once asked with what weapons the Third World War will be fought very cleverly and wisely: *Albert Einstein was once asked with what weapons the Third World War will be fought.* He replied wittingly: I am not sure which weapons will be deployed during the Third World War, but in the Fourth World War, they will fight with sticks and stones."

So many prophets have repeated the same thing. A prophecy should be a fixed statement that is unchangeable, detailed, and precise. Otherwise, it is not a prophecy. Real psychics give complete and accurate statements and do not and do not engage in vague talk.

In the end, no country with a nuclear weapon arsenal is willing to take the risk of exterminating most life on this planet at worst or alters the very foundation of civilization into a state of savagery at best. The words of the Mephistopheles in Goethe's *Faust* sum up the inherent demonic quality that *The words of the Mephistopheles in Goethe's Faust* sum up the intrinsic demonic quality that All that has been created, is worthy of demise. "The Blue Monks will not allow wholesale destruction of this world.

Anion (Seila Orienta) stated in 1997 that a world economic crisis will separate the wheat from the chaff, i.e., and usher a new era. Ultimately, it will be decided who will step across the narrow ridge and cross the threshold into the astral realm unharmed and pure. For there will be no war; however, times will become dire.

For readers who have not read Franz Bardon's first book, *Initiation into Hermetics*, I will conclude this chapter with the following words:

„Generally speaking, clairvoyance implies a second sight as it is popularly named, or the power of seeing, without the use of one's physical eyes, events taking place at a distance and in the past, present or future, or seeing deceased people. Very few authors describe this power from a psychological or any other point of view, and that is why it shall be out next task to study the phenomenon of clairvoyance very thoroughly. First of all, the magician will realize that there are various kinds of clairvoyance. The principle form is the inborn capacity of clairvoyance which its bearer has been granted whether in the invisible world already, or which he brought with him from a former into his present existence. This sort of clairvoyance is the best, but very few humans enjoy it, being born clairvoyant to such a degree that they can practice it immediately without any effort at all. The second sort of clairvoyance occurs spontaneously

and is, therefore, regarded as a pathological symptom. A shock in the case of severe illness also can cause the capacity of clairvoyance. This usually happens to people who lose their equilibrium as the result of a stroke, a nervous breakdown, a physical or psychic trauma, where clairvoyance will occur in a more or less distinctive form as a concomitance. This type of clairvoyance is naturally undesirable for the magician because it will sooner or later lead to a complete breakdown, which not only implies a total loss of this power but also is detrimental to the health and very often the cause of an untimely death. Clairvoyants of this kind are very pitiable indeed, even if their success should be convincing proof. This capacity belongs to all the persons who, having a mediumistic predisposition, were induced to clairvoyance by some beings. Nor is this kind recommendable to the magic practitioner, because people like this usually end up in a lunatic asylum. A significant number of persons who are taken to mental hospitals and who were meddling with spiritualism without a reliable guide can blame their hopeless condition on spiritualism, and it does not matter in the least whether the motives of this study were earnest intentions or mere curiosity or whatever else may have induced them.

Another form of clairvoyance that belongs to this group is the forced production of this power through drugs like opium, hashish, peyote, soma, and other similar drugs that alter consciousness. This will be without any interest to the magician because most of these victims will fall prey to the addiction of these dangerous drugs, which paralyze the ethical and intellectual faculties, the willpower, and finally, the nervous system, injuring the health as well as the development. Millions of cases were recorded in East Asia; however, they occur in significant numbers in the Western hemisphere as well as in all the other developed countries."

11.
The Third Catastrophe - The Global Economic Crisis

The above references to the Third World War are correct in a certain way, as they do suggest some truth about looming hard times that could be construed as a kind of war. I received the following answer to a question from mentor Ariane.

Ariane: "There's something in the air, everyone says. I feel it too. But no nuclear war, because in the end it destroys the planet Earth and that would not make sense, would it? Another catastrophe is looming. "

Hohenstätten: *"What do you mean by that? "*

Ariane: Ariane: „What happened two days ago? The big nuclear accident in Fukushima,[13] Japan, in March 2011 was the beginning of a looming global catastrophe. This nuclear accident cost countless lives swallowed up vast sums of money. The radioactivity is also spreading to the USA and around the world. This accident provided politicians with a stern lesson about what a nuclear war could cause. In comparison with a global nuclear war, this nuclear power plant accident constitutes a small example of the destructive nature of radioactivity. Whole areas have become uninhabitable for centuries."

---

[13] *The Chernobyl, Ukraine, melt-down of the nuclear core was quantitatively a greater disaster that Fukushima, although that is sometimes debatable. Since this nuclear accident happened in 1986, while the cold war was still in full swing, the reaction to this "lesson" posed to be not as poignant, although a cloud of nuclear fall-out affected the entire globe. Fukushima drove the lesson home, especially since Japan is a close ally of the USA and Europe, and the reactor is still spilling radioactivity into the Pacific.*

Think about the massive amounts of radioactivity spread by a nuclear war. Earth, or most parts would be uninhabitable for centuries. What purpose would Master Arion's mission played if humankind would perish? His initiatory works would have been written in vain, of our planet would be turned to radioactive dust bowl like the planet Mars. He did not endure all that suffering and mistreatment to reveal his wisdom to the world that would be destroyed a few decades later."

Hohenstätten: „*I concur.*"

Ariane: So, Master Arion and other great Masters (Brethren of Light) have ultimately altered destiny into something more conducive to our development on the path to adepthood. Bardon's mission has changed our future, and none of the so-called prophets have foreseen that.

Hohenstätten: And what did Master Arion do, aside from revealing his books of wisdom?"

Ariane: Ariane: He turned an impending world war into what would become a global financial crisis that will affect every country, even the smallest, and cripple the entire global economy. All nations will experience a complete collapse of their monetary systems and all banks. This time will be excruciating and austere, and this collapse that will bring disease, famine, and in parts of the world also governmental anarchy."

I always wondered how such a world crisis can happen, so I asked one of my uncles who works in an international bank. He sent my father an article by the German economist, Dr. Eberhard Hamer, titled *Der Welt-Geldbetrug* (Global Monetary Fraud), which I would like to discuss here. I discussed the present situation with my friends and family members, and all agreed that we are already in an incipient crisis. Many who understand current economics realize that the global economy is moving to an abysmal decline. Globalization has caused local economies worldwide to deteriorate. Our gluttonous economy will be crushed by its own weight.

A country has traditionally secured its money with gold reserves to balance between debit and credit. For many years, gold's value has increased at a steady pace until the 1970s. Today, countries depend on productivity to balance debit and credit since gold cannot be multiplied like economic output is growing since gold standards hinder a more durable economic growth. This is why banknotes were introduced, a practice that dates from the 17th century. However, the value of banknotes could be exchanged for gold or silver by the central bank at any time.

The gold standard would not allow economies to grow at a neck-breaking speed and increase monetary wealth exponentially. When gold-backed money, a country's wealth could only grow as fast as its government can procure mined gold once it becomes available. Since gold is a precious metal that is rare – 99% of earth's gold sank to the core throughout billions of years – it cannot be mined fast enough to enrich high finance exponentially. Today, voices are getting louder to advert to a gold standard practice.

Major financial groups and the Freemasons Rothschild and Rockefeller founded a private central bank called Federal Reserve System (the FED) through the Federal Reserve Act in 1913 with the right to issue its own money, which became legal tender and was initially guaranteed by the American central government. It was within this private bank that the world's gold reserves accumulated after the First World War (reparation payments from the Germany and repayments of war loans to US allies), resulting in many other currencies unable to maintain their gold standard and collapse in deflation. This became the first world economic crisis in 1929, the so-called Black Friday.

Over time, the central banks of the top forty countries in the world hold 29,500 tons of gold reserves (2019), and the US central bank alone holds 8,130 tons or 35% of the total. As mentioned before, gold used to serve as collateral for the dollar. However, since a more substantial part of the dollars was held as a reserve currency in the world's central banks, the United States could spend more dollars than it had on gold reserves. The international market needs US dollars to purchase commodities, which are traded on a dollar basis. The US dollar increasingly became the leading reserve currency in the world's central banks and dominated the world's economies. The US Government granted a private US bank the freedom to print as many dollars as it deemed necessary. While in the last thirty years, goods in the world have only quadrupled, while the money supply has increased forty-fold. Traditionally, money multiplication always translated into inflation, and inflation causes a depreciation of money.

Until the introduction of the Euro currency, the Deutsche Mark (short DM is also known as Deutschmark) posed competition to the dollar and became a preferred currency reserve of central banks around the world increasingly. Naturally, this competition hindered a US dollar dominion and had to be eliminated by abolishing the Deutsche Mark and integrating it into a European Central Bank. The Freemason German Chancellor Helmut Kohl manipulated politics to cast a decision in a small circle of powerful backers, without allowing the German population to vote. Through this decision, Germany lost a stable currency. Helmut Kohl stated that *"What would happen, should the community decide on such important matters?*

"The majority population would never have voluntarily sacrificed their solid Deutsche Mark.

No currency in the world today retains any intrinsic value basis whatsoever once the world's money was detached from any underlying material asset. To further devalue money, central banks unscrupulously print paper banknotes to increase the number of banknotes. Most people who handle cash daily, perceive their money has a fixed value owed to a manipulated perception of value through the skillful manipulation of exchange rates.

Oil is sold for worthless US banknotes since the oil trade is dictated by US dollars. Iraq's dictator, Saddam Hussein, wanted to sell his oil for euros. To avoid this charge, he was immediately declared a terrorist who harbored weapons of mass destruction. Saddam Hussein was a tyrant, but he never was a purported terrorist who threatened the world.

The US is increasingly forcing the rest of the world to supply it with goods in exchange for worthless money – a modern form of tributes. Ever-present greed and avarice across the globe coerce other countries to follow suit and play this game of monetary exponentiation. Dr. Eberhard sums up this financial fraud under the title:

Strategic Objective of Global Monetary Fraud
Dr. Eberhard Hamer

Anyone with some knowledge about financial manipulation can see from the outside, the original intention of US high finance was to dominate the US currency and thus be able to manipulate the US market at its own will. The private central banking system – FED – served this purpose. When US President John F. Kennedy introduced a law to nationalize this private financial system, he was assassinated. Individuals who tamper with this private money system of the US big finance will likely lose their positions, money, or lives.

In the meantime, however, the strategic goals of the US high finance have grown far beyond the national dimension. Their goal is the global private monetary system, which they have achieved mainly with the supremacy of their private dollar and its assertion to become a central currency reserve throughout the world. The next step would be the creation of a one-world currency - the "euro-dollar."

So if we want to prevent the manipulation of the world monetary system for the benefit of large private financial groups, and the misuse of money supply currencies in general, every currency must be protected against any public or private exploitation, against any inflationary and deflationary manipulation.

Preventative measures can certainly not be achieved by leaving the authority of a currency to the private high finance groups. Abuse, deceit, and exploitation of the world's monetary systems and an increase in money supply will work to the advantage of high finance.

However, experience has also shown that most governments misuse their currencies in the same way if they have the opportunity to do so, i.e., if they influence the central bank and its money supply policy.

It is, therefore, vital to turn the manipulations of the public sector and private wholesale finance into currencies that are so independent that private and public exploitation are ruled out.

Indeed, a gold-based currency is not as easy to manipulate as a mere quantity currency. However, the problems of any gold-based currency lie in the availability of gold, now that the US financial system has gotten its hands on most of the world's gold reserves. Any gold-based currency could become a winner and dominance over other currencies.

The only solution is a quantity currency. However, this quantity currency must not remain freely and arbitrarily determinable but must be oriented towards the neutral money target. The money supply must therefore not grow more strongly than the quantity of goods. The monetary sector must not again have inflationary or deflationary effects on the currencies and the global economy.

Avoiding such effects can only be achieved with central banks that are strictly neutral towards private and public influence and therefore be an independent entity that represents the "fourth power," as it were, and are not in private hands and cannot be influenced by governments. The original model of the Deutsche Bundesbank, before its castration into a Euro-Bank, came very close to being an independent, neutral central bank.

The forthcoming currency reform offers a unique opportunity to brand the perpetrators, their currency manipulations and their abuses, and thus to create general public approval for a central banking system that can no longer be influenced by either private high finance or self-serving governments. Such a feat would pose to be an opportunity of the century.

An independent central banking system could be prevented above all by the large financial institutions, which have already set the course for a new takeover of the next central banking and monetary system via the BIS (Bank of International Settlements), which has already been appropriated by high finance. For this reason, the population needs to be educated to show the population the danger of monopoly capitalism not only of the current currency system and a new monetary system.

The world's major currencies have grown so exponentially in a quantity that a small hiccup in the system could cause a catastrophic collapse and hyperinflation and will no longer have any real functional value for citizens. The exchange rate system of currencies is artificially maintained by manipulation and deception to allow money to have a genuine value exchange value. US dollars, printed by a private bank, have long ago shed all ties to material assets (gold) or other material valuables. The US Federal Reserve is purchasing tangible assets with increasingly worthless money for decades. The FED buys commodity warehouses, industrial complexes, real estate, and foreign corporations in friendly or hostile takeovers at any price. This way, it will maintain its position of power, and in the event of a crash, to still hold its trump cards in the form of tangible valuables.

Hyperinflation peaked in Nov. 1923 in Germany. The image above illustrates how worthless banknotes have become in the form of a one trillion note. (The number "billion" is a "trillion" in US numbering system: Million, billion, trillion as opposed to million, milliard, billion).

If one interprets the roadmap of the world's big finance correctly, one will realize the augment of a money supply to purchase valuable material assets throughout the world and monopolize its position. High finance circles know that its money supply increase will not go unnoticed and that at some point, the trust in the inflationary dollar will dwindle. At that point, the financiers have achieved a world monopoly status through the accumulation of tangible assets and can dictate prices.

If the dollar then collapses, the entire satellite currencies collapse with it, since the dollar is the base. Moreover, this is what every state now tries to prevent as much as possible. The only possibility is to come to world currency through currency reform. Nevertheless, even this is only temporary. Alan Greenspan, the former Chair of the Federal Reserve, has haphazardly stated in a speech *that "a fundamental dollar correction is imminent and that it would then be expedient to unite the dollar and the euro into the 'euro-dollar,' a new world currency"* (Amero). Something will happen to the dollar soon – or so Greenspan thought.

If the dollar and euro then were to become the world's only currencies, essential goals could be achieved to benefit the vast financial system of the USA: A newly created currency would void old currency debts and thus devaluing the creditors who still hold old currencies. A single euro-dollar type of currency possesses the same worth of twenty old dollars or fifteen old euros, and the old currencies have been devalued; accordingly, and if the creditors who hold old currency have been devalued, the game has been worthwhile for private holders of assets they procured through old currencies. The primary aim of high financiers in the USA is to create a world currency over which they, the US Federal Reserve, dominate.

The ongoing depreciation of money over the past forty years has not made ordinary people any wiser. Soon, the ship will run aground with full steam and constitute an abrupt end to our economies. The economy may show a brief respite only to collapse, In its final moments. A collapse of economies and wealth will lay the foundation that favors the everyday individuals who have been deliberately exploited by the financial elite everywhere around the globe.

There is a simple answer to the karmic reasons for a global downfall. Ideally, every country should strive to ensure the well-being of its citizens and not promote greed, avarice, and corruption by the upper echelon of society. Very few states embrace such ideals of social justice. This world is a transient place; there are birth and death, growth, and demise. Similarly, earthly happiness and material wealth grow and decline. The interaction of active and passive constituted the very fabric of our existence Life and is a learning process that serves our spiritual development. All states, large and small, as well as most of their citizens, display a universal consensus that applauses avarice, and accumulation of wealth, whether wealth is attainable by an individual or not. Credit card debt is at an all-time high, with the average US household $7100 in credit card companies. The average income individuals run up huge debts without thinking about the consequences of repayment with sometimes draconian interest rates. Everyone wants to revel in wealth.

People are trying to forecast what our future will hold for us. Everyone perceives something big and powerful is looming on the horizon. Many false prophecies have already been made, like the Y2K scare. Astrology is an influential business, as many people want to know their future. End time movies flood the movie theaters. Writers, movie makers, and novelists have become harbingers of the last days when some ultimate catastrophe will lapse us back into the Stone Age. However, the course of events will be different from the expected.

In peace-times, we are experience orgies of greed, corruption, and fleecing of the general population by the fantastically wealthy. Everyone seeks the pie in the sky, and avarice led to moral decay in our societies. Everyone wants more and more. Consumerism creates landfills that form imposing mounts, and pollution drives our world to the brink of destruction, yet our insatiable appetite drives us to want more goods.

Our world and cosmos are dictated by rhythm. What rises will fall, empires grow and perish, earth cycles around the sun in a year, the moon waxes and weans and we go from day to night and back to day. Daily we are confronted with sound waves, radio waves, or photons. Frequency dictates their qualitative aspect. It is only natural that vast economies will not grow infinitely, but will fall and collapse. Now is the time to heed all the alarm bells that warn of an impending collapse. We are blinded by movies and reality TV shows, silly sitcoms, sports, video games, pornography gluttony, and "stuff." We need more "stuff" to clutter our houses and apartments. We got to have the newest smartphone, the largest flat-screen HD television sets, gadgets through which we tell Alexa or Siri to turn off the lights or adjust the water temperature through a "smart" water faucet. We are like moths attracted to the flame, the ultimate flame of truth that will singe our wings and forces us to think on our own.

All the excesses we experience today constitute figuratively speaking, the beginning of the end of the world. Time-honored laissez-faire capitalism, the lack of equality, and libertarianism around has grown too fast and will collapse under their weight and perish. An incomparably tremendous transformation of events is underway. What we are experiencing as war and revolution, natural catastrophes, are merely the birth pangs of a new series of development for our planet and our human race.

Once humanity has endured and overcome the impending collapse, it will encounter a radical rejuvenation of the entire religious life, which we experience today as spiritual thoughts are shifting. Syncretism of dogma forms a universal set of religious beliefs. A renewal of social structures will produce a more balanced judicial system and equal rights. This time, Germany is undoubtedly destined to play a dominating role in this tremendous process of transformation in a much positive way that in the first half of the 20th century. For this reason, the three major works of Franz Bardon were the first published in Germany fourteen years after World War II. Germany will experience a significant runic-occult revolution and a synthesis of philosophical and religious literature. The light will spread around the world.

The intuitive reader knows and senses that infinitely higher concepts are at stake here: a new spiritual worldview that helps the souls to regain their inalienable rights that misguided religions, philosophies, and political systems have denied humanity to prosper. After the great catastrophe, this new world vision will finally overthrow this bankrupt materialistic heresy.

No one should resign in the light of what looms on the immediate horizon. As individuals, we must brace ourselves and look ahead to see the light at the end of the dark tunnel. Insightful individuals will see the coming times as an opportunity to free themselves from rotten, antiquated, concepts and ways of thinking and immerse energetically and purposefully in the service of a new age, whose faint rays of light will break through the dark clouds of doom.

Georg Lomer appropriately states that „Catastrophes *have and will trundle over humankind, to thrust the sparks of new knowledge and wisdom into the numb and imprudent mass of humanity.*

Only once erroneous ideas fall, the soul, the real human, matures to receive new things and become ready for the right spiritual paths.

Some will hold on to the belief of solid thrones and palaces – a storm will obliterate them, and all will crumble and turn to rubble.

You still believe that your selfish capitalist way, which bestowed a few individuals with unmeasured treasures while forcing the masses of hardworking individuals to toil in your factories with hunger wages, will grow indefinitely. There will, as the Bible states, come a time when we will hear howling and gnashing.

Do you worship money, this filthy mammon, and seek pleasure in amassing gold and shiny jewels? All currencies will collapse, financial crises will tear the fabric of society, the economy will be in ruins, and extreme inflation will devour fat bank accounts. The golden idol that you worshipped all your life will turn into a heap of rubbish and dirt before your eyes. All you valued all your principles will turn to dust and reveal you as a naked, old, and wrinkled hag. You will fall on your knees at the sight of your true self and regurgitate false ambition while you writhe in pain and anguish.

The ground you stand upon will dissolve from under your feet, and you will smash your greedy head and break and crush your bones in the abyss below. Surrounded by darkness, you will scream, yes, howl in pain and agony.

Any life that does not have higher and profound defenses will fall into darkness and despair. The great Arion, the spiritual demiurge behind the world organism, had to induce this situation that the souls that lost themselves will ultimately find themselves again within a guiding light. Only those, whose (material) passions died, shall be reborn a nobler soul.“ This statement correctly sums up the reason for this looming third catastrophe.

A Stock Market crash will induce an interest rate crisis, and once borrowers cannot pay interest anymore, the banks will collapse.

As a result, the real economy, corporations, the labor market, consumption, manufactories, and everything else will collapse. Naturally, massive unemployment will follow. While the first Great Depression of 1928 registered 25% unemployment in the USA, we will see double the rate during the collapse.

Once all the currencies throughout the world lose value, there will be many suicides, just like in 1929 in the USA, were once wealthy bankers who suddenly found themselves impoverished, jumped from skyscrapers. All the nations will have worthless money, non-functioning economies, and nothing to buy goods.

Food vouchers will be distributed again because hunger will be great. The formerly rich will line up with the poor in front of soup kitchens for food and medical needs. Gold coins and ingots will have less value than a loaf of bread. We will experience a new Stone Age, where a barter system will flourish. The big and powerful world banks will go bankrupt because there is no money of value left to conduct trade. Moreover, automobiles, aircraft, or ships will no longer be operational without oil production and working refineries. Whatever fuel remains will be prohibitively expensive.

Crime will also rise exponentially; one person will kill another for food to stay alive. Whole gangs of criminals will be sweeping through the country, and even otherwise, law-abiding citizens will become looters and thieves. Uprisings, revolts and civil skirmishes, and street battles will erupt in every country.

Naturally, emigrating into more sophisticated countries that have a sound social structure like Iceland, Denmark, and Norway, will not work, because even these countries will be in dire straits and will shut their borders to take care of their citizens.

Even knowing about the impending catastrophe, acquiring wealth, or material assets may make a hoarder a target for the have-nots. Karma is merciless but just. Saturn is the planet of judgment, and the cosmic judges will judge over humankind. There is only one way out of this malaise: Recognition and internalization of the cosmic laws of balance. Heaven and Earth are intimately espoused. And all earthly occurrences have their heavenly parallel, a cosmic origin.

The new state that will emerge after the catastrophe will be fair to all people and not just to a particular social class, party, or professional group. This crisis also motivates the creation of an ideal state and wholesome ethical socialism. Long ago, Peru was once a hear perfect state. Everyone had enough to live comfortably. These socially just principles still echo in today's Scandinavian countries and Iceland, who advocate the policy of equality social democratic principles.

Out of the rubble of our present society, a new state will arise like a shining Phoenix and blossom. Our earth will rejuvenate, and other laws will preside the future. Humanity must seek guidance through cosmic laws and principles such as *"That which is above is that* which is below." By bringing spirituality of the higher realms to earth, humankind will experience balance. After all, Akasha institutes the principle of equality, and that should be the goal of all state leadership. Instead of titles, dignitaries, and religious orders, the designate of brother and sister should be introduced.

People who do not understand the cosmic process will question the need for such a drastic learning process.

1. Karma: The sheer inertia of all the misdeeds, fraud, pilferage, racism, conservative laissez-faire capitalism, false religiosity, avarice, greed, hyper-consumerism, and the destruction of our environment have created a vast amount of negative forces that need to be balanced. 2. Inertia: Constant forward motion is a part of evolution. Standstill would constitute resignation and regression. 3. Self-realization: An individual's most ardent path is the path to one's true self. The ignorant masses will realize only retrospectively that our present way of life has led us to the point of no return. Most individuals sleep-walk through life, chase illusions and material trumpery, money, games and amusement, inordinate sexuality, and power. Our restlessness, and strive to overconsumption and amassment of goods will open the ground and swallow society. For this reason, hard-times must free us from our sleep state, from this materialistic spell. To awaken us, we must cease meandering through the dark and seek the light and strive for equipoise. The darkness of night still encompasses, and nobody recognizes that the time for redemption has long past and that a gaping abyss lay before us. However, a faint star twinkles in the heavens above announcing the return of a transcendental sun. Some will recognize this faint little star in the sky and understand: Some will notice this faint little star in the sky and understand: The world is full of subtleties and more profound than we believe it to be.

Overwork – "fast-paced" seems to have become a perverse motto in modern life – long hours, no or little vacation time (in many capitalist countries), pay-cuts, and fear of work performance assessments distract people from critical thinking and self-reflection.

Thanks to mobile phones and the internet, people will start work before and even after the workday has finished. Money problems, a plutocratic state that neglects its citizens in times of need, unemployment adds to this constant state of stress. We want that promotion into upper management and that smart thermostat, a „smart" faucet, the newest iPhone or tablet, designer fashion, and a granite kitchen counter. Our insatiable hunger compounds all these daily diversions for entertainment and competitive challenges. Religious demagogues of churches big and small misguide their faithful followers through misleading dogma and false belief and thereby stomp out the tiny spark of self-reflection that the lemming-like devout followers still possess. There is no time for introspection, meditation, philosophy, or appreciation for the little and simpler things in life. There is no time to realize that we are already sinking in the quagmire of materialism and notice the festering stench of decomposition. Most individuals have not realized that they are rotting inside and have become the walking dead. Retribution looms, and karma will lash out and humanity. Naked reality grins sneeringly at humankind; the Reaper knocks a people's doors and *exclaims: „Behold, it is I, this is my true countenance."* Hence, humanity will be driven away from excess materialism by force.

With the statement that *With the statement* that The wor^{ld} aches," the great 19th century poet-philosopher Friedrich Nietzsche, recognized that a striving individual needs something to bring about changes. Presently, we require assistance, an incentive to bring about changes. The deaf and blind sleepwalkers do not hear or see the message. Only agony and torment will awaken these masses from their slumber that will eventually allow them to recognize the follies and deficiencies of present-day societies. People will need a nod to be driven to see inside their souls. A minority of genuine spiritual seekers have seen the warning signs and have begun to work on themselves. They will look ahead at the difficulties ahead and will use these struggles as learning situations to reinforce their resolution to seek equipoise and advancement. In the coming times, billions of unemployed will populate the streets and, those who have experienced the painful consequences of our way of life through hunger, sickness, and violence will react and strive for improvement on an individual and global level. Lamentation around the globe will be profound once we will conquer the consequences of the great collapse, Divine Providence will granted all the opportunity to walk the path to spiritual and ethical betterment.

Inevitably, the great collapse and crisis must come, and it will strike hard and mercilessly. Many will perish, and many people will no longer cope with their new dire situation. They will break. However, those who do not admit defeat and continue to with their daily adversities will see the light that will flood through tiny cracks in a dark sky. Humankind will realize the grand plan of Divine Providence and recognize its customs, and the pure laws. They understand why they had to suffer and fathom the context of life's circumstances. Now, humanity is ready to impose true just laws and true unity without the boundaries of nationalism, pride, capitalism, and materialism. Those who recognize the astral realm as their true home will separate from those who pine for the past. The chaff will be separated from the wheat. There will still be those who prefer hell and materialism. Genuine seekers of the path, people do not want to lose their humanity, our highest good. For individuals who can see, the hermetic development will commence.

The pendulum of the karmic World Clock swings to a new beat, and all the momentary worries and fears are but a weak, cheap imitation of the forthcoming immersion in the vast symphony of cosmic events. This change is a renewal of unprecedented dimensions. All areas of public, superficial show life such as movie theaters, Netflix streaming, nightclubs, pubs, theaters, ball games, restaurants, concert halls, the entire music culture, pornography, car culture, parties and celebrations, enjoyment excessive partying, drugs and other pleasures will irrevocably vanish. Entertainment and cultural events will return differently, and once they return, they will bring new and bring time-honored hermetic traditions back to light.

12.
Master Arion's Plans

Years ago, I read a conversation between the German occultist, Dr. Musallam (Franz Sättler), and Arya Manas,
the supreme prince of Nuristan (Shamballa), in Musallam's book *Magic Bible* under the section *The Future
Eons.* I was quite astounded at what I read because Arya
Manas revealed what the future of Europe to Musallam.
After I had finished reading the article, I rushed to Anion to ask him about what I had read.

Hohenstätten

„Yes, Johannes, what Musallam wrote is right."

*„But how does he know?" I queried. "Musallam was not
a and advanced hermetic that he could have visited the
temple Bit-En_Nur (Shamballa) or converse with Urgaya."*

*„That is correct," Anion said, "but you keep in mind that
Musallam personally knew Franz Bardon, who had giv-
en him the information about this material."*

„All right, then the text comes from Master Arion?"

„What do you think?" Anion grinned

*Just to be clear," I asked Anion a bit shaken," the text
clearly states that a transformation is not a gradual process?"*

*I pulled the book out and turned the pages until I reached
the chapter I had read and read out loud:*

*"The changes will not occur overnight," Arya Manas
said, "and the whole world will not suddenly be transformed as if by magic. Let it be said, most of humanity
still lives in a state of animalism, a wretched society of
half-animal beings who are sadly still afflicted by lower*

passions, vices, and illnesses (i.e., sociopathy and psychopathic tendencies). These wretched beings will not go to sleep one night, only to awake the next day as blessed, angelic beings dwelling in a paradise-like world. No, the great change, this last great catastrophe, will take place in a completely different way. It will have its beginnings decades before that time of such a change and continue for several centuries beyond. Yes, the change has actually already begun. The Great War has placed causes and created conditions on earth that cannot possibly last. The seed seeds of new, violent events have been planted. The next decades will bring an accumulation of such events: New wars small and big, and revolutions. These coming events will nevertheless stir up nations and their citizens from the ground. The end of the 20th century will lead to the formation of a great European empire.

A vast empire in Europe? I (Musallam) interrupted curiously. And which nation will be the ruler? What form of government will this empire have: A republic or monarchy? 'The latter,' replied Arya Manas, deliberately ignoring my first question. 'Such an empire can only be a monarch.

And who will be the monarch? What nation, what dynasty will he come from? I pressed on.

'His name will be - World Peace,' Arya Manas replied, 'and his kingdom will stretch from the Ural mountains to the Pillars of Herakles. This monarch will hail from a Nation that toppled from being a world power to having to obey to the victors' whims. That is all. I may now reveal to you this. But, once you have learned to read the stars, the rest will be revealed to you.

Further along, Musallam states that the new European empire will only constitute a transitional empire to be replaced by a unified global empire. To clarify this state-

ment, I again ask Anion, who then told me the following: To explain this statement, I asked Anion, who then told me the following: The Akashic oscillations of the earth are amplifying as we speak. The chaff will separate from the wheat in a Third World War. However, there is still time for redemption to avoid wholesale annihilation and a resulting dystopian global society.

There will come a time, where a new world will develop, in which nature and culture will coexist in better harmony. A Godhead will sound a quabbalistic tenfold-key to effect earth in a way that new just laws will be created by just and compassionate people will strive to live in harmony with each other. All this may sound like a utopian phantasy today, but rest assured, humanity in generals will refine, and with it, our planet as well. Noble thoughts – noble deeds that are a karmic law. Hell on earth will finally become a purgatory.

A transformation of the physical elements will occur. The material plane will become more transcendent and subtle.

That means that the astral beings, like the beings of the other elements, become visible. Today's churches will one day become museums because owed to their stubborn, and fundamentalist stances, world religions will exist only in history books. After the war (catastrophe), the Hermetic sciences become a guide for new or reformed world religions. Humanity will mature, become refined, and Hermeticism will have room for other faiths. In time, the earth and other planets will transcend to a more astral state. Life spans will increase to centuries. Then, anyone will have enough time to reach equipoise. Individuals will no longer "die," but willingly and consciously exit their bodies. Once we reincarnate, we no longer lose our consciousness of our experiences in the astral realm. However, some time will still pass before we reach this state."

Anion's wife, Ariane, once stated that *"Still, smaller wars and skirmishes will flare up occasionally for the next 600 years. But, the shock of the third catastrophe will sit deep in the collective psyche of humanity that in time firearms, grenades, mines, and other means of modern warfare will be abandoned in favor of time-honored weapons such as the sword and shield to wage wars. The weapons of the old represent the fairest methods to wage a fight. Cowardly weapons such as machine guns of sniper weapons will be viewed as dishonorably to wage wars.*

All churches and such institutions as we know them today will disappear, and then a leader, a giant spirit, will again appear to usher in the new age. This leader will be a balanced spiritual world ruler who will justly guide and direct the destinies of all nations.

Alas, before this happens, genetic engineering experiments will create a monster of a sort and cause diseases, like the ones that Jan Hanussen already has predicted. Genetically modified creatures will tread on our earth.

But, what happens to us, the students of Bardon's hermetics?" I asked Ariane.

„Master Arion said to me in a conversation that he would not abandon his true students. He cared for them and prepared everything so that they would survive the Third Catastrophe relatively unscathed to continue their development here on earth. Provided that a student treads the path with the necessary acuteness and proper attitude."

„But why does Anion write about an actual World War III?" I queried Ariane.

"War as a nuclear war, as Anion writes, has been misinterpreted. War can also be translated to struggle or

global catastrophe. And you know, Johannes, every battle you fight leads to victory."

Verachte nur Vernunft und Wissenschaft,

des Menschen allerhöchste Kraft,

lass nur in Blend- und Zauberwerken

dich von dem Lügengeist bestärken,

so hab ich dich schon unbedingt."

Johann W. von Goethe

*

Scorn all reason and science too,

Humanity's highest Good,

Allow deceit and sorcery infiltrate,

Once lies undergird your mind,

13.
How to Prepare for an Economic Collapse

Protecting yourself from a collapse due to all adversity is quite challenging. A catastrophic failure of the economy will happen without much warning, and preparations will become impossible. In most crises, people survive through their knowledge, wits, and by helping each other.

Here are steps you can take now to prepare for a potential collapse.

Make sure you understand basic economic concepts so you can see warning signs of instability. One of the first signs is a stock market crash due to war, pandemics, or natural disasters. An economy is a frail construct so that it will fall apart quickly

As for cash, it may not be useful in a total economic collapse because its value might be decimated to hyperinflation. Stockpiles of larger gold bullion may not help because they would be difficult to transport if you needed to move quickly. Small coins might be easier to transport. However, in a severe collapse, gold may not be accepted as currency. But it would be good to have a stash of $20 bills and small gold coins, just in case. During many crises, these are commonly accepted as bribes.

In addition to your regular job, make sure you have skills that you'd need in a traditional economy, such as farming, cooking, or repair. I am not a proponent of firearms, but if you can, get a handgun and learn how to use it.

Make sure your passport is current in case you'd need to leave the country on short notice when there is still time. Research target countries now and travel there on vacation, so you are familiar with your destination.

Keep yourself in top physical shape. Know necessary survival skills, such as self-defense, foraging, hunting, and starting a fire. Practice now with camping trips, and if you can move near a wildlife preserve in a temperate climate. That way, if a collapse occurs, you can live off the land in a relatively unpopulated area.

You need to stockpile canned food, a grill, fuel, or a fireplace in the backyard (if applicable). You will need a source of water. A rain barrel might work well or large canisters of water. Several water filters are useful as well. You need a couple cast iron pots and pans if you cook over an open fire. Also, don't forget antibiotics, first aid kit and manual, hygiene products such as toothpaste and toilet paper.

Remember: After a total collapse, there will be a run to grocery stores. Isles will empty within a few days. Demands for fuel are not met so that cars won't run, and no new food supply will be shipped. Once power is out, the internet collapses. Nothing will work. We will be back in the early 1800s, except people back then knew how to cope and live well.

Conclusion and Dedication

Since I am just a small wheel in the clockwork of the occult, I would instead like to dedicate this book to a woman whom I would call one of the greatest women I had the distinction to befriend. Throughout the time, I had the distinction of knowing her, she has been my friend in need and a great mentor, without whom I could have never established my publishing house or written many books that I offer.

Ariane, whose life has more than a hell, and who nevertheless mastered all the Tarot Cards, lived silently and entirely unrecognized. She was the one who inspired me in many ways in life and bestowed upon me much rare and unknown information to write my books.

Hohenstätten

Ariane

Bibliography

Ach, Manfred. Das Nekrodil: Wie Hitler wurde, was er war. Arbeitsgemeinsch. f. Religions- u. Weltanschauungsfr.; Edition 1 (9. November 2010).

Allen, Gary & Larry Abraham. None Dare Call It Conspiracy. Dauphin Publications; Special edition (January 30, 2013).

Bardon, Franz. Practice Of Magical Evocation. New Leaf Distributing Co Inc (September 1, 2017).

Bender, Hans. Zukunftsvisionen, Kriegsprophezeiungen, Sterbeerlebnisse. Piper Verlag GmbH (Mai 1988).

Berthold, Will. Die 42 Attentate auf Adolf Hitler. VMA; Auflage: 12., (2007).

Brandler-Pracht, Karl. Die Sintflut kommt wieder! Ein Nachweis der Wiederkehr der grossen Weltkatastrophe auf Grund astronomisch-geologischer Feststellungen, Berlin 1920.

Daim, Wilfried. Der Mann, der Hitler die Ideen gab. Wirtschaftsverlag Ueberreuter; Auflage: 3. (1. Januar 1994).

Eckart, Dietrich. Der Bolschewismus von Moses bis Lenin. Zwiegespräch zwischen Adolf Hitler und mir. Hoheneichen, München [1925].

Gregorius, Gegor A. Der Weg ins dunkle Licht.

Gregorius, Gegor A. Politik und Loge.

Griffin, Des. The Missing Dimension in World Affairs, South Pasadena, CA, Emissary Publications, 1976.

Hanussen, Erik Jan. – Der Untergang New Yorks. Der Untergang von New York: Roman. Köln: Smaragd-Verllag, 1990.

Hemberger, Adolf. Pansophie und Rosenkreuz Teil II [in 3 Bänden]. Selbstverlag, Gießen 1974.

Hitler, Adolf. My Struggle (Mein Kampf). Free Thought Books (April 20, 1922.)

Lomer, Georg. Die Prophetie der Natur. BoD - Books on Demand; Auflage: 1 (27. Oktober 2014).

Lomer, Georg. Kommende Weltkatastrophen.

Rauschning, Hermann. Hitler Speaks: A Series of Political Conversations With Adolf Hitler on His Real Aims. Kessinger Publishing, 2006.

Rüggeberg, Dieter. Geheimpolitik, Bd.2, Logen-Politik. Rüggeberg, D; Auflage: 3., (1. Januar 1997).

Sebbottendorf, Adam. Bevor Hitler kam: Urkundlich aus der Frühzeit der Nationalsozialistischen Bewegung. Munich: Deukula-Grassinger, 1933.

Serrano, Miguel. The Golden Thread: Esoteric Hitlerism. Wermod and Wermod Publishing Group (August 15, 2017).

Serrano, Miguel. Adolf Hitler: The Uultimate Avatar. Forefathers-Art.com (2017).

Other Books Available at Hermetic League Publishers

Talismanology and Mantram Lore
by *Franz Bardon/Seila Orienta*

112 pages; softcover
For the first time (hermetically) charged mantrams are revealed here, which promise pervasive successes with the necessary maturity, balance, and purity.

The Book of Anion
by *Seila Orienta*

40 pages; softcover
This brief treatise demonstrates the true perception and knowledge of the material existence in the light of hermetic development. Furthermore, the text reveals the many errors, entanglements, trials and tribulations in the student of the hermetics encounters

As Above So Below

by *Seila Orienta*

216 pages; softcover
This autobiography displays an honest account of the life of an adept. Seila Orienta speaks candidly and openly about important and interesting milestones in his life.

The First Lesser Arcanum

Franz Bardon's Secret Key to Divine Realization
by *Johannes von Hohenstätten*

64 pages; two pictures and two graphs; softcover
The 1st lesser Arcanum has not been published until now. This Arcanum enjoys a prominent place between the first and the second Tarot Cards. Up to this time, the 1st Lesser Arcanum has been taught and practiced exclusively in the astral plane.

A Practice Guide

Supplemental Advice on Franz Bardon's IIH Course

by *Seila Orienta*

44 pages; softcover
This little guide should serve the student with supplementary hints and explanations through the course of Initiation into Hermetics

The Golden Book of Wisdom

The revelation of the 4th Tarot Card According to
Franz Bardon
by Seila Orienta

44 pages; one picture of the 4th Tarot Card; softcover
This card represents the qualitative form of magic and even the theorist will be astounded by the hermetic philosophy contained therein.

Alchemy

A description of the 5th Tarot Card
by Seila Orienta

44 pages; one picture depicting

the 5th Tarot Card; softcover
This Book depicts the introduction of the Fifth Tarot Card that was labeled "Alchemy" by Franz Bardon.

Hermetic Genesis

An Adonistic Tale
by *Seila Orienta*

2nd Edition; 48 pages; softcover
This novella informs the reader about the tasks of the Blue Monks, Urgaya.

The 72 Names of God

by *Seila Orienta*

28 pages; softcover booklet
 The seventy-two passages pertain to pure Divine ideas which and creation.

Shiva Samhita

by *Anonymous/Johannes von Hohenstätten*

72 pages; softcover
The Shiva Samhita is the most important classical treatise on Yoga. This work has its origins in Eastern Tantric practices.

Unveiled Archives of the Secret Sciences

Volume I: The Bible of Adonis

by *Wilhem Quintscher. Hermes Trismegistos*

140 pages; softcover
This first volume of the "Revealed Archives of Secret Sciences" is a precious pearl of hermetic literature. Not only because these works are of ancient Egyptian origin and were written by Hermes Trismegistos,

Master Yeshua:

The Life of Jesus Christ

by *Johannes Hohenstätten*

63 pages; softcover
This biography of Christ - the greatest adept of all time - delves into written accounts, unmentioned in other studies of Christ. This work utilizes countless information from unknown ancient writings.

Sexual Magic

by *Gregor A. Gregorius*

72 pages; softcover; 5.5 x 8.5 in
This little book is part of a series of study guides that Gregorius has written during the post-World War I period called the Weimar Republic. These days, the 1920s, proofed to be a very fertile ground for diverse lodges and occult and magic teachings, especially in a large cultural center as Berlin.

A Delineation of True Sexual Magic

by *Johannes von Hohenstätten*

140 pages; softcover
This book is the first hermetic compendium of all previously published books, writings, and manuscripts on the subject of the "Magic of Sexus". The reason for the publication of this work was the fact that much of what has been written on this topic consists either of nonsense, perversities, falsifications and deliberately twisted opinions about sexual magic.

Books Available in other Languages at Hermetic League Publishers

Im Garten Luzifers

Der Werdegang eines Suchenden

Buch I & II

Ein Roman von *Peter Windsheimer*
410 Seiten; softcover

Georg Steingarten erlebte die Grausamkeiten des Ersten Weltkrieges als junger Leutnant in den Stellungsschlacht-en an der Westfront. Seine Erfahrungen, die Unmen-schlichkeit und das Leid während der Kampfhandlungen, ließen ihn am Sinn des Lebens und des Daseins zweifeln. Nach einer schweren, fast tödlichen Verwundung stürzte der junge Leutnant Steingarten in eine dunkle Depres-sion. Selbstzweifel, tiefer Hass gegen sich selbst, gegen die Schöpfung und den Schöpfer grub er sich tiefer und tiefer in eine aussichtslose Lage.

Come sopra, così sotto

La mia vita come adepto

Autobiografia di *Seila Orienta*

Tradotto in italiano da Sara Sudano
Questa autobiografia mostra un resoconto della vita dell'adepto. Seila Orienta parla apertamente di impor-tanti e interessanti traguardi della sua vita come gli incontri con l'ordine magico, le visite alle sfere, ai domi-ni di geni negativi, gli studenti di Orienta e la Bardon League che fondò negli anni '80 e alcune precedenti in-carnazioni dell'autore. La prima parte del libro è pura-mente autobiografica mentre la seconda parte descrive le intuizioni che l'autore ha raccolto durante la sua vita ermetica.

Il libro d'oro della saggezza

Rivelazione della Quarta Carta dei Tarocchi secondo Franz Bardon

di *Seila Orienta*

Tradotto in italiano da Cristina Ventrella

Per la prima volta nella storia della letteratura dell'occulto, la quarta carta dei Tarocchi del grande Ermete Trismegisto viene svelata e descritta. Oltre a questo, ci sono degli esercizi di concentrazione e meditazione sconosciuti. Per di più si fa riferimento alla differenza tra magia e misticismo, così come ai pericoli del sentiero unilaterale. Infine, al completamento di questa quarta carta, troverete una tecnica di congiunzione con il Dio universale, signore della sfera solare. Nella Cabala, questo signore è definito 'Metatron'.

El Primer Arcanon Menor

La Clave Secreta de Franz Bardon hacia la Realización Divina

Por *Seila Orienta*

Traducido por Ana Rosa Gómez Obregón

Únicamente los iniciados genuinos del hermetismo conocen verdaderamente el significado que tiene el Prmer Arcano Menor para el desarrollo mágico del adepto principiante. Hasta ahora, el verdadero significado simbólico de esta carta fue pasado directamente del Maestro a sus estudiantes más dotados. Este Arcano ha sido desconocido fuera de los círculos de iniciación hasta el día de hoy. Franz Bardon otorgó el conocimiento de este Arcano a Ernst Quintscher, el hijo de W. Quintscher.

Alquimia – Los Misterios de la Piedra Filosofal

Revelación de la 5ta carta del Tarot
De acuerdo con Franz Bardon

Por *Seila Orienta*

Traducido por Vbollatti

Este libro retrata la "parte frontal" o introductoria de la práctica alquimica en varios pasos sin las encriptaciones míticasde los antiguos, más en la línea del estilo de Franz Bardon. A pesar de que para el terórico, alguno de los escritos que contienen esas páginas pueden parecer abstractos y contradictorios, pero el practicante encontrará un amplio conocimiento en este libro.

Assim Acima, Como Abaixo

A Minha Vida Como Um Adepto

Uma Autobiografia por *Seila Orienta*

Traduzido por Gilson Cardoso de Arruda

Esta autobiografia expõe um sincero relato sobre a vida de um adepto. Seila Orienta conta honestamente e de forma aberta sobre importantes e interessantes fases marcantes em sua via, tais como encontros com ordens mágicas, visitas às esferas, domínios dos gênios negativos, discípulos de Orienta e da Liga de Bardon a qual ele fundou nos ano de 1980 e algumas encarnações anteriores do autor.

O Livro Dourado Da Sebredoria

Revelações sobre a quarta carta o tarô

De acordo com Franz Bardon

Por *Seila Orienta*

Traduzido por Daniel Bueno Iost

O livro dourado da sabedoria apresenta um texto conciso e direto sobre a manifestação da quarta carta do tarô, além de fornecer dicas de como alcançar essa importante energia. Que é de suma importância para a iniciação das ciências herméticas.

O Génesis Hermético - Um conto Adonístico

Por *Seila Orienta*

Traduzido por Micaela Mendes Nóbrega

Este conto dá a conhecer ao leitor sobre a existência e o desempenho dos Monges Azuis, de Urgaya, Shambala Mestre Yoshuah (Cristo) e Mestre Arion (Franz Bardon), que não foram conhecidos até agora. A Génesis ou a criação é mostrada da perspectiva hermética. Embora este livro contenha simbolismo e metáforas, conta claramente a génese de nossa existência e o nosso propósito neste universo.

Alquimia - O Mistério da Pedra Filosofal

Por *Seila Orienta*

Traduzido por Ravi Martins de Almeida Sampaio

Este livro retrata a "folha frontal" ou porção introdutória da prática da alquimia em vários passos, sem as mistificações codificadas dos antigos alquimistas, mais na linha do estilo de Franz Bardon. Embora, ao teórico, algumas das escritas contidas neste livro possam parecer abstratas e contraditórias, o praticante encontrará vastos conhecimentos dentro destas páginas.